LADDERS 2019 RESUME GUIDE

Marc Cenedella

LADDERS

www.theladders.com

or visit us on Facebook:
https://www.facebook.com/LaddersHQ/

D0066724

LADDERS

Marc Cenedella: Founder and CEO

1. Introduction

Two decades of advice packed into 90 minutes

Why are resumes hard?

I was in my second year at Harvard Business School, and I was struggling with my resume.

I'd put hours of effort into making sure it was perfect: rearranging bullet points, changing words around, inserting a new accomplishment, then deleting that accomplishment, and re-thinking it before re-inserting it again. Accomplishments big and small from jobs recent and past went through this endless cycle of include, delete, repeat.

Every time I made a change, I'd show my newest resume to fellow HBS students and staff. They'd inevitably have a new batch of comments and suggestions for improvements.

So it would be back to the laptop for more updates, effort, and worry about whether or not I was doing this right, and secretly wondering whether or not all of this was a waste of time. I was up against clever students who had been at Goldman Sachs, Microsoft, or McKinsey, and they were going to get hired first, weren't they?

I was out of my league, out of ideas and out of patience with the whole resume-writing process.

Even the spelling of resume is a mystery -- do you really need to type résumé? How do you make those weird characters anyway?

It did seem odd to me that the students and professors at America's top business school were so confused about resumes. Sometimes, the advice given by one classmate today directly contradicted the advice I'd been given last week by another. To be honest, it kinda seemed like a lot of them were making it up as they went along. If all those bright lights from shiny backgrounds were confused, how could anybody get it right?

I guess understanding that question appealed to me, because I've made it my career. In the two decades since my own struggle with resumes in business school, I've gone on to specialize in jobs, careers, and career advice. My firm, Ladders, has provided feedback on millions of resumes and studied the results of tens of millions of job applications. We've researched what's worked and what hasn't. And we've distinguished between the essential and the useless advice.

Here's the truth about your resume: it's a relatively straightforward business document that any professional can craft themselves, correctly and competently, in a few hours, without a lot of drama. With a plan, a good understanding of the goal you want to achieve, and the necessary, simple instructions for putting it together, writing your own resume is a business task you can readily accomplish on your own.

The goal of this book is to put that plan into your hands over the next hour or so.

I'll provide you with the tools, tactics, and tricks you need to get your past experience into an effective resume. We'll review the right format for structuring your past jobs into a job history. We'll tackle the best wording and how to phrase your past achievements. We'll highlight the most effective way to use your professional summary to put your best foot forward.

I'll provide you the guardrails to make the process easier to understand, easier to do, and easier to survive. I want to limit the amount of time you find yourself worrying whether you ought to write "Out-performed expectations" or "Exceeded expectations". Doubts like these are not a good use of time, but can feel weighty when you've got resume anxiety.

As a result, you'll get a resume almost as good as if you'd hired a professional resume writer to do the work for you. If after reading this guide, you decide to go ahead and hire a professional to assist (always my advice, to be honest), you'll be a better, more informed, and more capable client.

If you're feeling up to trying the "do-it-yourself" route, I'll show you, step by step, how to create an attractive two page resume in a modern, effective format, in this format...

FIRSTNAME I. LASTNAME

firstname.lastname.2019@gmail.com

Address - City - State - Zip Code

(212) 555-1212

GENERAL & OPERATIONS MANAGER

COO • VP, Ops & Admin • Country Manager • Senior Operations Director
Business Development • Revenue Generation • Strategic Planning • Relationship Management
Led Business Growth • Increased Productivity • Reduced Costs • Effective Recruiter
Team Leadership Award 2018 • 3x Executive of the Year • Promoted Early • Public Speaker

WORK EXPERIENCE

Current Company Name, Inc., New York, NY   April 2015 - present
Chief Operating Officer
Leading Contract Manufacturer in Service Industry

- Increased productivity by xx% after taking over supply...
- Delivered 3 new distribution centres on budget...
- Improved results for delivery success goals by xx%...
- Optimized sourcing strategies resulting in 8 new manufacturing...
- Produced savings of $xx million across operations, maintenance...
- Reduced defects by over xx% by implementing large-scale...
- Generated a xx% on-time performance increase by streamlining...
- Exceeded market share goal by x points through reduction of...

Prior Company, Inc., Lake Forest, IL.   Jan 2011 - April 2015
General & Operations Manager
$14 Billion Global Manufacturer and Distributor

- Maximized profitability, generating over $xx million annually by implementing...
- Accelerated delivery of new technologies to reduce headcount by 16%, adding...
- Achieved xx days reduction in closing cycle time by overseeing analysis of...
- Sold 3 data centers, generating $xx million in cost reductions...
- Decreased technical and operational costs by xx% by creating strategies...
- Orchestrated xx% revenue growth by developing and executing...
- Streamlined logistics resulting in $xx million in annual cost savings...
- Grew net income by more than xxx% by overseeing...

Middle Company, Inc., City of Industry, CA   2004 - 2011
Promoted early from Product Manager
General & Operations Manager   May 2007 - Jan 2011
- Added 310 basis points to customer satisfaction scores by...
- Gained xx% efficiency improvement by implementing...
- Contributed to a budgetary saving of $xxM through the acquisition...
- Expanded role to supervision of 5 critical distribution locations...

Product Manager   Sep 2004 - May 2007
Operational Product Management
- Awarded patent for osmosis system that reduced costs by 67% in core manufacturing...
- Eliminated 12% of components through product redesign while maintaining quality...
- Introduced a pricing strategy that saw a xx% rise in increased...

First Company, Inc., San Antonio, TX   July 2001 - Sep 2004
Product Manager
Strategic Product Management at Global Industrial Manufacturer
- Saved 23% on operating costs by implementing ordering...
- Minimized customer complaints and increased sales by xx% by restructuring...

EDUCATION
Grad School University Name   2001
Master's in Precisely Specific Degree, Houston, TX
- Winner of award, distinction or honor
- Member of club, society, or organization

Undergraduate College or University Name, Austin, TX   1999
BS/BA in Precisely Specific Degree
- Winner of award, distinction or honor

PERSONAL, PATENTS, AWARDS, TECHNOLOGIES, KEYWORDS (OPTIONAL)

Team Leadership Award 2018, Certified Manager (CM), Conflict Management Certified (CCM), 3x Employee of the Year (2018, 2016, 2014), Process Improvement Category 2015, JustFood ERP, NetSuite, Prodsmart, IQMS ERP Software, Integrify, Deskera ERP Software, Risk Mitigation, Research & Development, Profit & Loss, Lean Manufacturing, JIT, TQM, Purchasing & Supply Chain Management, Change Agent, Production Cultivation, Production Harvest, XtraCHEF, Parsley, FiiX, ProLease Maintenance, SiteDocs

Firstname I. Lastname

In addition, we've uploaded 73 separate resume templates that cover fields from Accounting to Media to Manufacturing to Technology, and many more, on Ladders' website here: https://www.theladders.com/resume-examples

You can also find additional resources at the home page for this book: https://www.theladders.com/career-advice/resume-guide

I start this book with the 'how come' rather than the 'how to'.

It's a different approach from other career writers, who begin their resume advice with margins and font sizes. I've found that professionals like you are more powerful when they understand the 'why' first. And **American** professionals -- being the best educated, brightest, and most successful business people in the history of our planet -- are at their best when given the tools to understand the reasons behind the task, rather than just commanded to do the task.

In fifteen years of writing America's largest career advice newsletter, I've discovered that if I take the time, respect your intelligence, and share the purpose behind the advice, then that advice becomes much easier to follow, and much more likely to be put into practice. To be honest, all this career advice stuff is not really that complex, and after a few years in the industry it's amazing how obvious it feels. I hope to pop the bubble, dispel the myth, chase away the monsters under the bed, and reveal the little man behind the curtain, of resume writing.

It's just not that difficult, and you're going to be able to understand it all just fine. For the typical professional, you just haven't had a lot of time or inclination to think about writing a resume, and nobody in management, HR, or recruiting has taken the time to explain it in a straightforward way.

Now if you're very itchy to get going, you could skip the 'how come' and jump ahead about ⅓ of the book to the section titled 'What is the floor plan of the modern resume?' But then you won't be getting your full money's worth from *Resume Guide* even though you already paid me for it. The choice, my friend, is yours.

The recommendations throughout this book are targeted towards a professional with 10 to 25 years experience. For those with fewer than 10 years' experience, you are better off with a 1-page resume, and I will address how to do so in the relevant spots. And for those with more than 25 years' worth of experience, or those earning $500,000 per year or more, three pages may sometimes be appropriate. This is not the correct book to address the specific and rarefied needs of that segment of the working population, and you're far better off working with executive search specialists on crafting the appropriate resume for you. In addition, this book is targeted towards private sector professionals and does not cover the specialized needs of military, government, or academic employees.

The resume advice in this book will take you about an hour or two to read, probably two to four hours to do, provide months of benefit in reducing your resume anxiety, and years of advantage in structuring and managing your resume over the course of your career.

As with any "do-it-yourself" project, the key to success is to not get in over your head. I've trimmed some of the specific expertise and more advanced tactics that I have advocated over the years in order to make this advice something that you can take action on today. This simplified version of my best advice is tailored to be achievable, by you, on your own. If you've got the commitment, moxie and willpower, here we go!

Oh. One more thing. As we begin this journey together, let's ditch the pretensions right away -- in the practical, 21st century, American business world, we spell resume **without** the cute little French lines above it.

C'est la vie!

Your resume is a professional advertisement, targeted toward your future boss, with the goal of landing an interview for a job that you can succeed in

The title of this chapter is "Your resume is a professional advertisement, targeted toward your future boss, with the goal of landing an interview for a job that you can succeed in."

To a certain extent, the title of **every** chapter in this book is "Your resume is a professional advertisement, targeted toward your future boss, with the goal of landing an interview for a job that you can succeed in." It could be the title of this book, the last line and the first line of every chapter, and every caption in between.

That's because so much anxiety, worry, and nonsense have been wrapped around resume advice over the last few decades that sensible people like you have come to believe that resumes are mysterious, unknowable, semi-magical parchments that mere mortals will never understand. But of course that's not true.

Writing resumes is not complex. It's not mysterious. It's not magical. It doesn't require as much luck or talent as writing a romance novel, a great song lyric, or a funny best man's toast.

Done right, writing resumes is kind of boring in form and format. The whole point is to allow you and your achievements the chance to shine. As a piece of business writing that hopes to achieve a business goal, it is actually far less dramatic or confusing than many people's fears have led them to believe.

Your resume will be an effective professional advertisement:
- Your professional summary will act as headline or billboard, boldly communicating who you are and what roles are right for you
- Your work experience will describe the companies for which you've worked and the jobs you've had with a brief, effective format
- Your accomplishments at those jobs will be delivered via 25 bullet points, each of which will have a success verb and number, making effective supporting argument for your candidacy
- Every element of your resume will work to underscore and support the message you've broadcast in your professional summary about who you are and what roles are right for you

As in any business task, writing this business document profits from knowing what's needed, and what's not needed.

Throughout this book, we'll be focusing on what you **do** need:
- Understanding who you are and what you want to do next, realistically, concisely
- Reminding yourself that the goal of writing a resume is to get you an interview for your next job, nothing else
- Using the professional summary to communicate "what I'm looking for" to your audience
- Writing about your successes, not your duties and responsibilities
- Using numbers to quantify your successes
- Including keywords that touch on the most important skills and capabilities in your field

Equally important is understanding that some advice on resumes is flat-out wrong. Here are the things you **won't** need to worry about in reading the resume advice in this book:
- Using a thesaurus to find obscure verbs
- Detailing each project you've ever worked on
- Including jobs from more than 15 years ago
- Agonizing over font choice
- Clever design with multiple columns, graphics, or colors other than black

Some friends -- let's call them the "Global 1%" -- who are blessed with great, good fortune will let you know that resumes don't require this much effort at all. The top one percent of global professionals -- those acquaintances who hail from the Harvard / Yale / Princetons, or the Google / Facebook / Apples of the world -- will tell you not to push it so hard. All they had to do was list out their past fantastic brand name institutions and job titles on their resumes with no supporting achievements, numbers, or persuasion. And they've continually gotten ahead in their careers. "See?" they might say, "all that effort applied to outlining successes and outcomes is working too hard and seems too pushy."

Because they've regularly landed on ever-higher plateaus of success without breaking a sweat, their resume advice differs dramatically from that outlined in this book.

And there's a reason for that. The experience of being admitted or hired by Harvard, Google, or the others, and making it through several years at those rarefied institutions, is itself a signal of a type of high performance that is its own form of persuasion. They've expended thousands of hours on arcane and difficult topics in a rigorous, competitive, extraordinarily demanding environment over many years in order to acquire the stamp of approval from a globally respected brand. And they tend to apply to other globally respected institutions whose managers went to those same schools and employers. Their proven ability to exceed performance requirements, combined with the brand prestige accumulated over centuries or decades, are sufficiently persuasive on their own. If you're fortunate enough to be in the Global 1%, then you might find my resume advice unnecessary in your own career.

But for everyone else, what works for people in the Global 1% might not be effective for you.

Other helpful friends at the other end of the spectrum may tell you that this structured resume advice is all nonsense. With a far more lackadaisical attitude, they got their last job with a resume that barely filled out a page. It was enough that they knew the hiring manager from college or had met the recruiter on a flight!

And it's true, "any old" resume can get you "any old" results. Even a bad resume often won't **prevent** you from getting a job if you've got the talent and the performance and the connections.

But a good resume, in our format and following our advice, will help you create more opportunities, with more future bosses, leading to more chances to land a terrific new job. For the best results, putting the best foot forward with the best possible resume maximizes your chances, your outcome, and your income.

As a reminder, you can find more information, templates and examples online here:
www.theladders.com/career-advice/resume-guide
www.theladders.com/free-resume-templates
www.theladders.com/resume-examples

What's a resume do?

"Your resume is a professional advertisement, targeted toward your future boss, with the goal of landing an interview for a job that you can succeed in."

Let's dive in more deeply.

"Your resume is a professional advertisement"

Your resume is an advertisement. The product it is selling is your work effort over the next few years. For the typical member at Ladders, where incomes range from $100,000 to $500,000 per year, that can represent millions of dollars of value. A product with this large of a price tag merits a good advertisement.

If you've sold a house, or a car, you know how a well-written ad can generate a lot of phone calls and interest. It's the same for resumes, but in this case, a resume is a **professional** advertisement, seeking to inform and attract buyers of professional talent. To reach and entice them, you'll showcase your professional qualities, features, and performance.

A resume is not a personal, or personals, advertisement -- it's not a place to preen or cleverly display how much of a catch you are. It is not a social advertisement indicating your social or marital status, or seeking to ensure your inclusion in the Social Who's Who of your city.

It is an **advertisement**, not a Product Manual of You. not an exhaustive transcript of your past work experience or schooling, and definitely not a first-person bio or autobiography. You want to steer away from thinking that a resume is a precise or complete history of all your past work experiences, a catalog of prior responsibilities, or an inventory of your past staffing levels and budget authorities.

Like any good ad, a resume provides your contact info (it's surprising how many professionals goof this up with casual or non-professional email addresses). And like an ad, it shows others have worked with the product before by highlighting the brand names in your past. It serves as a discussion starter for interviews. And it provides a basis for references that will come later in the process.

Unfortunately, a resume is also a place for you to make **disqualifying mistakes** or **exaggerated claims** that will come back to bite you later. Typos, simple professional mistakes, or untruthful data, can torpedo your chances. If your resume is too many pages too long, has strange formatting, or has an unprofessional filename, you'll raise eyebrows.

If you write "Fluent Spanish and Chinese", but meant fluent Spanish and a smattering of Chinese, it can trip you up in interviews. If you list 'SQL', 'Excel', 'Mailchimp' or other software, but can't answer the basics about them, it will call into question your competence and your integrity.

"Targeted toward your future boss"

Perhaps the biggest mental hurdle in writing your resume is getting over the fact that a resume's target is not you, and that a resume is not about pleasing you, or even being the way you'd like to think of yourself most.

In fact, there's a certain extent to which the resume does **not** reflect the man or woman you are. When you think about yourself as a full-fledged human being, you don't only consider your professional achievements, but also your family, friends, religious affiliation, college ties, hobbies, and other attachments, motivations, and cares.

Because these other areas of your life tend not to have a written document -- kids, thankfully, don't require a resume before jumping on you, and mercifully, we don't have to hand over a two-pager to gain admittance to our churches or synagogues -- we tend to overestimate the extent to which our resume should reflect 'the whole person', and 'everything about who I am.' It's often our only chance to sum it all up!

As a result, a successful resume may be even a little bit disappointing for you, personally. Because it is the single most common written document we have about ourselves, it's relentless focus on just one, narrow, cold, and business-focused aspect of your humanity can leave you dissatisfied.

Other times, you may find your focus drifting toward audiences that are more important in your thoughts, than they are in reality. A resume is not a good place to settle scores, puff up one's non-professional achievements, or engage your inner professor. You should not use the scarce space on your resume to justify your past decisions to your colleagues, address an admissions committee in your head, or seek the approval of your peers. It's purpose is not to explain your job to a general audience, your daughter's 5th grade class, or college friends who went into other fields.

A resume is targeted at the specific people who can grant you an interview for a job, and then persuading them to actually do so.

"With the goal of landing an interview"

Your resume is not going to land you the job all by itself. That's simply asking too much of a resume. Perhaps in the technological future, there will come a time when a few minutes after hitting "send", you'll receive a note from your future employer with a neatly formatted offer letter and a 10% raise, but that time has yet to come.

So if not an offer, then the goal of the resume is to land the interview.

If it's a draining process for you to be sending out resumes, it's an even more draining process for the people on the receiving end. Their full-time job is to sift through the deluge to find the pearls. That can mean reviewing hundreds or thousands of resumes, most of which, sadly, range from the wholly inappropriate to the wildly unrealistic.

While there's a temptation to stand out with puffery, exaggeration, and hyperbole, it's far better to stand out with facts, realistic expectations, and a sober assessment of your achievements. When hiring managers are looking for directors with 15 years experience, they're not looking for people who are managers with less than five years experience, and they're not looking for executives who are also targeting jobs that require 25 years or more experience. If you are a precocious prodigy, or greatly down-shifting, there are ways to manage that in your resume and communications, but the core idea remains -- hiring managers want to hire people with about the skills and experience they are looking for, with a track record of past accomplishment.

There's really no need for fudging facts, there are plenty of bosses looking for someone just like you. For the poor souls on the receiving end of the flood of resumes, you want to stand out for the right reasons.

"For a job that you can succeed in"

The internet has created a deluge of applications, resumes, and spam for HR people and recruiters. It really has been a double-edged sword for them. For every perfectly qualified rocket scientist that applies for the Rocket Scientist job at

SpaceX, there are a hundred dishwashers and broom-pushers who throw in an application as a lark. It's really unfortunate.

To land a job you can succeed in, it's helpful for you to know who you are, what's available in the market for people like you, and how you can apply yourself to future opportunities.

I address planning out your next step in *Ladders 2019 Careers Guide*, but the short version is that you'll most likely want to make a progressive step in your career with steadily increasing duties, responsibilities, staffing, and goals. For 90% or more of the professionals that we've worked with at Ladders over the past two decades, that's their ambition (along with a shorter commute, nicer people, or a more interesting set of challenges).

In any case, you want to have a good, plausible idea of your next role. By focusing your efforts on jobs within a range around that role, and not shooting too low or aiming too high, you can generate the most success for your efforts. Knowing who you are and who you want to be and then hammering home those points, specifically and repeatedly, is your path to getting selected.

2. The four audiences for your resume

Who is my future boss?

Odds are that you'll be hired by a stranger.

Most Americans end up being hired by strangers, in fact. It's one of the strengths of the American system. Rather than being dependent on who you know, or who your parents knew, or who your parents' parents went to college with a century ago, in the USA we try to hire the best person for the job, regardless of social, family or ethnic backgrounds.

Now, given the math of most industries, it's also the case that you'll probably be hired by a friend of a friend, or a friend of a friend of a friend. In any city, and in most fields, the likelihood that you "know someone who knows someone" is actually quite high.

But at the moment you create your resume, your future boss is a stranger to you. The better you understand your future boss' mindset, and the people and systems she has helping her, the easier it will be.

Your resume has four audiences to please. There's a **23-year-old screener** with a couple years experience in HR who makes a first pass through resumes to determine if basic qualifications are met. There's a **recruiter**, who is either an outside search consultant, or an internal HR employee, who reviews the screened resumes to assemble a shorter list for the boss. There's the **hiring manager** herself -- while she is the decision maker with regards to the hire, it's best to think of her as a client of the recruiting process. And finally, sitting alongside the entire workflow is the company's HR computer system, called an **applicant tracking system** -- understanding how the world's computers read and relay your resume significantly reduces your chance of making mistakes.

These four audiences determine whether or not you make it to the next step. The specifics and the configuration of these roles and responsibilities are as varied as any human organization, but this typical arrangement captures the essence. Each of these audiences has a different need from your resume, and a slightly different goal for what they are trying to achieve in the process. It is important that you not assume that they are like you, or have your sensibilities, preferences, or capabilities. We will review their incentives, behavior patterns, goals and outcomes individually, and it is most effective if you can address each of their needs in your one resume document.

Resumes are advertising, and advertising sells

Even the dictionary gets it wrong.

Resume, spelled with or without those little French lines above it, is defined as a "summary" or "a brief account of one's professional or work experience and qualifications, often submitted with an employment application."

The dictionary even points out that resume comes from the French word résumer, meaning to summarize.

But that dated definition does not reflect the US employment market in 2019. There may indeed have been a genteel time when we lounged about, sipping tea and collecting cash from peasants, when this advice was useful. Summarizing who you were, and who your parents were, was enough to secure yourself a place at the King's Court.

As recently as fifty years ago, this summary of your schools, clubs, and connections was enough. At the time of old boys' networks and old school ties and Old Grand Dad bourbon for expense account lunches, this made sense. Resumes, and their European equivalent, the *curriculum vitae* (CV), came out of academic backgrounds before they became part of the world of professional work, and did very little to sell the people they were representing. Selling, in fact, was considered low class and kind of cheesy.

In our modern world of work, in which hustle, merit, and achievement are what matter, you'll be assessed by strangers that didn't go to the same "old school", aren't from the same "old family", and don't care about your "old boys".

You need to sell. You need an ad.

But because we're not accustomed to writing advertisements about ourselves, we can feel confused. The sensible advice your parents gave you against bragging and self-importance in social settings seems to conflict with expectations in the professional world. And indeed, it's important to separate those personal virtues from effective business communication. In the context of the 21st century American business environment, you have a duty to yourself and your family to accurately convey, and negotiate for, responsibilities and compensation at the level appropriate to your professional development. A fair and rational assessment of your achievements, and the ability to communicate those achievements to a business audience, are important to your success as a business person.

An ad that sells you and your abilities is expected, necessary, and modern. Relying on the dictionary to tell you that it is OK to merely summarize is a good way to get left behind with the "olds".

User guide vs. ad

It's useful to illustrate the difference between these approaches using the iPad Pro as an example. The iPad User Guide is several hundred web pages of detail and summarizes everything you need to know about operating and maintaining your iPad or iPad Pro. Importantly, everything in there is **true**. It's not opinion or puffery or exaggeration. The iPad Pro User Guide summarizes the privacy and security features, shows you how to use Apple Pay, and explains to you all the different ways that Siri can misunderstand your spoken commands. Overall, it provides a vast amount of data and information about the latest iPad.

Here's the homepage for the latest User Guide for the iPad and iPad Pro:

iPad User Guide

Welcome

What's new in iOS 12

> Set up and get started

> Basics

> Siri

> Apps

> Apple Pay

> Sharing

A different approach is taken by this still photo from a TV ad for the iPad Pro. It is also "true", but delivers its message in a completely different way:

It shows you what a professional user can do with the iPad Pro -- in this case sketch an architectural drawing based on client feedback. Other iPad Pro ads show users creating videos, taking notes, and editing presentations. It's not opinion or puffery or exaggeration, you really can do all those things on your iPad Pro.

While both are "true", one is far more effective at actually selling the iPad Pro.

The user guide is, by far, more comprehensive in its exhaustive cataloging of the iPad Pro's capabilities.

But by making it easy for future users to see, literally, the **benefits** of the iPad Pro, the TV ad does a better job at getting users to say "hey, I could use one of those." And that's what drives sales.

Similarly, a resume that **sells** is better than a resume that **summarizes** when it comes to the important task of getting your future boss to say "hey, I could use one of those!"

When you write a resume that summarizes, you're focusing on what it felt like to **be** you. You were there, you experienced all of these things, and your memory of the time is laden with great detail of those events and adventures.

Conversely, a resume that sells makes it easy to see, literally, what it feels like to **hire** you. To manage you. To succeed as a boss because you've joined their team.

When you show your future boss the **benefits** of hiring you, rather than summarizing the experience of being you, you make it that much easier for them to say "hey! I could use one of those!" and call you in for the interview.

How to sell the benefits of hiring you

I was speaking at Target headquarters a few years ago to one of their leadership councils. To get to the next level at Target, employees needed to apply for an internal job with a complete resume and go through a hiring process similar to the external one. I shared the story of selling your benefits to your future boss.

During the Q&A after my talk, a woman raised her hand and asked 'well, what if you have a really boring job?'

Which got a big laugh.

So I asked, 'well, what's the boring job?'

And she said, 'Logistics.'

'Well, why do you like doing that?'

Her eyes lit up: 'it's such a challenge to get all the items for sale from one place to another, it's like a big puzzle.'

'And why do you like doing it at Target?'

'Well, we're always opening new stores, and I love working at the company, so I'm looking for even more interesting challenges.'

'And what do you hope to do next?'

The excitement fairly jumped out of her voice: 'Move up to the next level of responsibility and run a small region of warehouses.'

'Well,' I said 'it doesn't sound too boring to me, and it's clear this is really your interest and your passion...

...it sounds like you're a logistics professional who loves solving ever bigger puzzles and challenges in moving and managing goods around the country. You appreciate the chance to do it at Target because the company's always growing and you're learning more each time. And your next desired role is a little bit larger so you can keep learning and growing in this, your chosen profession.'

'Yes,' she said, 'when you put it like that, I guess it's not so boring.' Which got another big laugh.

And, in fact, your career and your aspirations are not boring to your future bosses. While the details of logistics, or any field, might be a snoozefest for your friends, family or kids, they are desperately interesting to the future boss looking to hire a logistics expert to help her solve her problems for 2019 and beyond.

And the same goes for your field. What gets you excited about your field are the same things that get your future boss excited. Because for both of you, it's a career, a calling, and the path to future glory. For both of you, the desire to move up requires a passion for just the type of dreams about the future that got my audience member in Minnesota excited.

Even more, you need to understand that for a boss, assembling a team is not just part of the job, it's part of the thrill. It might be similar to the feeling you get when you score your secret weapon in the fantasy football draft or buy a new pair of shoes that look great for the fall. There's an emotional response you have -- 'this is terrific! I know exactly how I'm going to use this!'

That's the same feeling you want to create in your future boss. He's building his team and has a variety of positions to manage. Knowing that you'll fit the bill gives a thrill and he'll say 'terrific! I know exactly how I'm going to use this person!'

What the logistics expert at Target and I had stumbled onto was her 'elevator pitch' -- a concise four sentence statement of what you're looking to do next. It's called an elevator pitch because you're supposed to be able to rattle it off in the time it takes an elevator to go to the top floor. It's valuable because it forces you to think very clearly about what you're doing and why you're doing it.

Now I suppose she could've said "I'm seeking a role of progressive advancement upon which I can further my career goals. By leveraging my expertise in intercontinental logistics for multi-hub efficient distribution environments, I would hope to be assisting in improving the efficiency and desirability of internal distribution practices at a global multinational company."

And for a particular type of very brainy operation, that could actually work wonders. But most people's eyes will glaze over before the end.

Interestingly, though, those aren't the words, that isn't the tone, she used when she was standing there in front of hundreds of her colleagues. Instead, she spoke from her heart, about how she really felt. And the enthusiasm was contagious. All the words were hers, and when she shared them with us, she was mighty. She was powerful. All it took was her being herself.

And while we cover crafting your elevator pitch in full in *Ladders 2019 Careers Guide*, the short version is that an elevator pitch is composed of four sentences or phrases:
- Say what you've done in the past -- a brief description of yesterday
- Say what you're doing now -- a brief description of today
- Say what you like about it -- a brief enthusiasm for your work
- Say what you'd therefore like to do next in your future -- a brief description of tomorrow

The more you can make these four sentences sound like a conversation over beers on Friday night, the better. I know we all start using that 'corporate' sounding voice when it comes to describing work, but the more you can make it feel like something you might say in conversation to your grandmother or cousin or college buddy, the more effective it is.

Thus, it's not "I'm a saleswoman" but rather "I'm a sales management professional looking to lead a 100+ person sales organization, and am particularly interested in opportunities leading sales teams going through the transactional-to-relationship-selling transition."

It's not "I'm an engineering manager" but rather "I'm an engineering manager who has been team lead for the past few years on our ecommerce shopping cart experience, where I love completing the sale and driving customers through checkout, I'm looking to expand my horizons to owning the entire development process."

And it's not "I'm a finance guy" but rather "I'm a finance guy who enjoys rationalizing finance teams in multi-unit businesses and creating metrics and operating procedures that partner with the business to drive understanding of the underlying levers of growth."

When you are specific and concise in your elevator pitch, you make it easy to transform your future job goals into resumes, cover emails, phone calls, or whatever form or format your career planning may require. Selling the benefits is not about including **all** the facts -- just the ones that get your future boss excited.

The single biggest trick

When it comes to resumes, you want to tell people how it felt to **be** you. But your audience wants to know what it felt like to be **your boss**.

Writing your resume is a unique experience. Even though it concerns you, writing a resume is not like writing a diary. Although it covers a time period in your life, it is not how you experienced those days and years.

When we sit down to write a resume, we often start with writing what it felt like to be you -- this school was followed by that education was followed by this first job was followed by that next promotion, and so forth.

You share, in bullet point format, the stories that are interesting to you, the drama that was involved in getting here, and provide a compelling plotline to your own life story. For you, each job, each accomplishment, each bullet point, was an adventure, a battle, a triumph.

This is the easiest version of your life story to tell because it feels like something we've been doing all our lives. It's the version of the story that you're familiar with, the version you tell your folks and friends, your new acquaintances and your oldest college buddies.

And once you get going, it gets easier to write about yourself and start filling the page: your jobs, your duties, your promotions, your projects, your transfers, your staff. And when you get to editorializing -- the achievements "despite" budget shortfalls, or "in the face of" industry declines, or "with minimal support," it can feel like a vindication, a validation, a victory.

And the factual and emotional weight of each bullet in your resume become like little movies you can play back in your head about "that time when…", or "my first job out in San Antonio…"

But the emotional weight of each line of your resume has very little correlation with the professional weight your boss will assign to it. And the little career movies you are replaying in your head may have no impact on your goal of landing interviews.

If there's one **trick** I'd like you to understand about getting your resume right, it's this: **your resume is not about you**.

Sure, it's made up of your achievements, background, experiences and credentials, but it's not **about** you. It's **about** the benefits your future boss gets from hiring you.

You resume is not about you. Any more than the iPad ad is about the transistors, and code, and chips inside. While those are the materials that make the magic possible, the iPad ads entice you to buy the magic, not the bill of goods.

Similarly, your resume is about your future boss' needs and the benefits she'll obtain by hiring you for the role.

A boss is looking for output, not input. A boss is looking for outcomes, not duties and responsibilities. A boss wants to know the end of the story, the bottom line, the score at the end of the game, not the feelings you had while delivering them.

In fact, if you're looking to move up in your next job, your future boss is two levels above your current role. So your ability to understand their needs, predicaments, hopes, requirements, and best guesses for the role are understandably limited by your own limitations of experience.

That's one of the reasons why even HR pros who have been hiring for decades have a tough time with writing a resume (and with many other parts of the job search process). Much like doctors are the worst patients and attorneys are bad clients, HR people have tons of experience in hiring others, but almost no experience in hiring someone like themselves or their boss. Being a great buyer has very little to do with being a great seller.

Gaining the required distance to write about yourself in the form of a professional advertisement is difficult. Seeing yourself as a product is hard. Portraying yourself not as "you", but as the sum total of all the labor your future employer is purchasing is something you don't often do. We don't know precisely who the audience is. We don't know what we are supposed to say. We're not sure how we are coming across. And we feel sheepish about bragging so blatantly to an imaginary herd of peers in our head. The novelty of the experience, and the oddity of the perspective, can leave you feeling adrift, unmoored, a bit lost in the landscape.

Writing a resume is not like how you think of yourself in any other part of your life.

So the balancing act of mastering your own emotional response to past achievements, and the ability to weigh those objectively so that you can convey the professional value of each of those achievements and its worth to future employers, is the most important "trick" to resume writing. It's a new skill. You'll get better with focus, awareness, and practice.

To bridge this gap, let's start moving toward crafting your resume by doing a little exercise. It's a kind of charades or guessing game, I suppose... can a stranger understand what you want to do next by tearing off the top third of your resume?

Can a stranger understand you from the top third of your resume?

"What does she want to do next?"

When your future boss picks up your resume, he needs to know the answer to that question before he puts it down -- who you are, what you do, and what you're good for.

Take the first page of your current resume and rip it off -- I mean, literally rip the top third away from the rest of the page or cover the rest up with your hand. If this is all of your resume that a stranger was given, would that stranger be able to tell me -- and would they be able to repeat back to you -- what job you're seeking? Without any discussion with you, would it be as clear to them as the iPad ad is to the viewer about its use?

The answer, for your sake, and for the sake of the effectiveness of your resume, **must** be "yes", and we will go into some detail about precisely how to construct this top third. Because the first thing that all of the audiences reading your resume want to know is this: "Does this gal, or guy, want this job that I have to fill?"

Do not assume that because you're a Director, it's obvious that you want to be a VP in the same field. Do not assume that it's obvious you want to work in the same industry, in the same role or specialty or function, in the same size company, or in the same type of situation. And that's because for every person like you who wants to zig this way in your career, there's another person with a similar background who wants to zag in theirs.

Much as the iPad ad is bold with demonstrating what you can do with the iPad, and doesn't assume people will understand the uses from the packaging alone, the top third of your resume is your billboard.

Obviously, given that you've spent the time to create a resume and send it to them, they know you want **"a"** job. But do you want **their** particular job? Is it something that you've done before? If so, did you **like** it? If so, do you want to do it again?

So it's best to spell it all out, explicitly and obviously. Unless you put it down in writing on the top third of your resume, they won't know what you want do. It can be a total mystery to someone who hasn't met you yet, which is pretty much the definition of who's reading your resume.

Make it easy for your four audiences to understand what you are looking to do next -- they are so buried under an avalanche of applications and work and information overload, that it is far better to make it very clear to them, from the very beginning, precisely what it is that you're looking to do. Make it easy for them, or you'll make it hard on yourself.

1st audience: the 23-year-old who screens your resume needs your help

The first audience for your resume is a junior HR screener.

The internet has made life easy for HR at the same time it has made life impossible for HR. Being able to communicate instantly with anyone on the planet felt like a present from above when the internet first came online. No longer would resumes have to be printed out! No longer would job descriptions have to be printed in newspapers! The internet was going to make communications instantaneous, free, easy, and ever-present.

Which is exactly what happened. Except that by making the internet instantaneous, free, easy, and ever-present, HR's life actually got worse in some ways. No longer did people have to think through whether or not their resume was really right for a job. No longer did only a few, or a few dozen, qualified people apply for a job. No longer was every resume received attached to someone who was polite, professional and accomplished.

Instead, HR was suddenly buried in unqualified applicants. Google receives one million resumes per month. A typical job posting on major job boards attracts 1,000 or more applicants. Searching through even small resume databases returns hundreds of resumes for niche roles.

All of which means that HR had to find some way to deal with the unprecedented volume of resumes they needed to review. The solution, at scale, has been to hire and train a relatively junior person to sort through the resumes first. Whether their title is HR coordinator, HR assistant, Recruiting Specialist, or any of the dozens of other flavors of titles that have sprung up, this person is typically a year or two out of college, personable, and interested in a career in HR.

But they are not an expert in your field or industry.

This **junior resume screener** is comparing your resume to a list of skills, titles, or companies that he or she has been given by the recruiter. Overly clever resumes or cutesy positioning can really kill you with a junior screener. Because they don't understand the nod and the wink that comes with writing "Chief Bottle Washer" when you really mean "Co-Founder", attempts at humor can be lost on them. For these reviewers, the choice of phrases in the professional summary is especially important.

The typical junior screener will work on all of the jobs across all of the recruiters on his or her team. That means that she might be reviewing technology resumes today, sales resumes tomorrow and operations resumes next week. He will be called upon to screen the applications to an individual contributor job today, a senior executive job tomorrow and a mid-level manager job next month.

This wide variety and assortment of jobs and resumes in their workflow means that a junior screener is almost always making assessments in an area in which they have little personal or professional experience. In fact, with only a year or two out of college, they typically have little to no experience in **any** area, not just yours.

Despite this, the reason their bosses put them to work is that the volume is so great, the work of sorting and screening so mind-deadening, the hours saved so compelling, that it makes sense to delegate the work to someone other than the more experienced recruiters. At the same time, because the level of fidelity with which a screener can effectively review resumes for job applications is fairly low, their bosses will provide them with guidelines that tend to be over-generous, over-inclusive, and over-shooting the mark, rather than the opposite.

It's not an uncommon tactic in any field: have the most junior folks do a first cut before handing the work off to the more experienced people on the team. So that might mean that if the role is a purchasing agent role, the screener is assigned to throw out any resumes that obviously aren't in purchasing, or have only managerial experience in the past decade. Or if the job required is database designer, the first cut will be to throw out all non-technology resumes, and perhaps sort by the ones that mention database most prominently.

The result of having this 23-year-old screener in the process is that you absolutely cannot assume that they know anything. Even the most basic features of your role, your job, your industry, may be new, or only recently learned, by the person assigned to screen your resume.

You may think this is unfair. After all, you've spent years or decades honing your craft, learning the intricacies of your trade, becoming an experienced contributor, and perhaps even an expert in your field. With all of the time and energy and effort that you've expended on becoming a highly paid professional, it would seem that the least a company or executive search firm could do would be to have someone age- and experience-appropriate review your resume to determine where you might fit best. You might feel it's a matter of simple decency and respect.

And you may even be a bit justified in thinking this way. Socially, it does seem unfair.

But as an advertiser, this happens all the time. The car company that invested hundreds of thousands of worker hours into developing new technology, the software team that put in hundreds of person-years to ship the new tool, the cosmetics company that hired dozens of professors to conduct years of research to make a better product, all face the conundrum that when it comes to presenting their efforts to consumers, the effort isn't always immediately appreciated.

However wonderful you think your product is, it is still important for you to present the product in a way that the audience understands.

So whether it's Apple's demonstrative ads for the iPad, or the way Disney sells you on the expression on your kids' face, or Toyota sells cars by focusing on the look you'll have on **your** face, advertising needs to ignore the feelings of the professionals who made the product and connect with the consumer who wants to buy it.

So however unfair it may be, the reality of the matter is that the modern HR process will land your resume on the desktop screen of a junior employee. To get to the next step, you need to construct your resume so that this junior person with no experience in your field will easily find words and phrases that match the screening criteria they have been given.

This is why your professional summary is so important. You'll use well-chosen words and phrases to describe who you are and what your background and capabilities are. The words you choose mean there are words you won't choose, or be able to fit, in your summary. In many cases, the absence of certain words (manager or individual contributor, back-end or front-end, performance-based or branding) can be as important or determinative as the presence of others.

It is also why it is important for you to not jump immediately into the arcane details of your field or your profession in describing your positions. Because the voice in our heads is often, itself, coming from a point of view of being an industry professional, it can assume that the audience knows all about the basics, and even the intermediate details, of a field. For the junior screener, this can leave them adrift as they search for the presence or absence of the basic criteria their boss has assigned them to suss out of your resume.

Finally, the reason we keep the resume to two pages is that length itself is a hurdle for the screener. The candidate who has sprawled their information across four, five, six pages or more has made the screener's job of finding keywords or buzz phrases that much harder. The likelihood for confusion is greatly increased when you leave it to a junior HR person to determine which of your many pages, and densely packed paragraphs, they should prioritize in their review.

2nd audience: seven seconds is all that recruiters spend on your resume

Ladders' research reveals that the typical **recruiter** spends just 7.4 seconds on a first glance of your resume. We've got a small window to grab the attention of this important second audience.

Recruiters are the original "people people". They are *literally* people persons, in that they do people for a living. So the way that a professional like you might inspect a technology, a law, a marketing campaign, a shipping schedule or a balance sheet, is the level of care, insight, diligence and enthusiasm a recruiter brings to understanding the person behind the resume.

'Recruiter' as a term covers both external recruiters -- third party brokers who are hired to fill a specific role for a hiring manager or company -- as well as internal HR people who do recruitment for a living at a specific company. In addition, at some smaller companies or divisions, you'll find that an HR generalist handles recruiting along with other HR duties.

The actual work of recruiting is telling stories. We **measure** a recruiter's success based on the number of hires that they make, but the actual **work** of recruiting is storytelling.

Having spent a lot of time with our recruiter customers over the years, it's fascinating to hear them talk through a resume out loud. They'll spin a tale about the person behind the resume. As they hold the resume up in one hand, or scroll through it on screen, they'll explain out loud -- either talking to themselves, or to me -- something about the history of this person, how they got to where they are, and, if it's self-evident, why they did what they did. They'll tend to fill in the little gaps with guesses and intuition based on all of their past experience about what similar people have done in the past -- being people people it's usually the rosiest, most positive, most upbeat spin possible.

When a recruiter gets a job order from a company, or from a hiring manager, they have a limited amount of time to do the search and return a list of half-dozen to a few dozen candidates to the hiring manager. In order to generate this list, they'll need to review perhaps a few dozen or so resumes themselves. So recruiters and HR people place a premium on being able to find the information that they need to know quickly.

Even specialized recruiters who work only in a particular type of role -- sales, or marketing, or software engineering -- find that they have to work across such a broad range of sub-categories that they can never truly grasp the nuances of your work.

Fortunately for them, they don't have to be experts in your field. They only need to understand enough about the work to understand the skills, and outcomes, and responsibilities of the different roles they're handed. And the way they do this is by taking a broad, "first cut" approach to the stack of resumes their assistant, or software, returns to them: they'll be looking for the right keywords, companies, and achievements on your resume.

Because recruiters often need to recruit in a wide variety of fields -- far more than is humanly possible to comprehend -- they are often called upon to be champions at 'fake it till you make it'. As long as they fake it well enough, the hiring manager and candidates such as yourself might never realize that the recruiter has only a surface knowledge of the field. Far from being a form of deceit, this important skill allows a recruiter to specialize in recruiting without having to master the underlying subject matter -- a benefit to everybody.

If a recruiter is looking for a individual contributor sales person, he may focus on finding phrases such as "achieved 117% of quota", "President's Club", and "delivered $1.7 mm in bookings in 2018." When he sees "hired and managed a team of 12", "delivered regional sales quota on target", or "established company's first sales award program", he knows that he is looking at the resume of a sales manager, not an individual contributor.

Similarly, if a recruiter is looking for an engineering manager, she will want to see words and phrases such as "hired a team of 11 front-end engineers", or "established code review practices", or "implemented Agile methodologies". If she sees instead "learned Go to implement concurrency in our systems", or "tasked with re-implementing legacy software in an AWS environment", or "coded front-end applications for publishing division of media company", she'll know that she is instead looking at the resume of an individual contributor.

These behaviors are no different than anything you do in your field of expertise when searching for information. There are subtle clues and hints as to whether a document, or article, or paper is the right level of depth, addresses the type of concerns for which you need answers now, or if the product literature targets the problem you're hoping to address. In fact, as a modern knowledge worker, you probably spend most of your days using your judgment, experience and insight to make fine-grained distinctions between sources and types of information for your work output.

Because recruiters are not practitioners in your field, they'll start broad, and narrow their search as they go, often as a result of conversations with the hiring manager.

A recruiter looking for an individual contributor in sales, may get feedback from the hiring manager after the first round of discussion that they're actually looking for someone who can do the work remotely, is independent-minded enough to achieve success in that environment, and has experience dealing with companies in the consumer packaged goods industry.

Another recruiter may discover after her review with the client that the desired person should have experience in Java, as the role requires a lot of work in maintenance mode, and is specifically looking for someone with back-end systems experience.

In each case, the recruiter will then narrow the words or phrases he or she is using to screen resumes.

What this means for you is that your "fear of missing out" is unjustified. Because the first two levels of resume review and screening are looking to create a slate of candidates with a slightly wider focus than the hiring manager will ultimately find useful, they are doing your expansive thinking for you. The tendency to make your resume over-broad by loading it down with an ever-more-far-afield variety of even tangentially related keywords, buzzwords, accomplishments, work efforts, and responsibilities, works against you in these drill-down exercises. You should resist the impulse.

It is not only that an over-broad approach is unneeded, it is also dangerous. By watering down your message, you reduce the punch you can deliver when you are exactly on target. For example, if you're the individual contributor sales person above, but stretch minor managerial tasks into actual managerial accomplishments on your resume -- 'helped to craft and deliver the company's new policies on commission escalators' when all your involvement took place with your old college buddy over lunch -- you can inadvertently signal to the screener that you're not actually within the target they're looking for.

Or if you're the engineering manager, and you spend too many lines discussing actual coding projects and cutting edge tech personal exploration -- 're-wrote company's social media pipeline in Go' -- again, you risk unintentionally setting off the screener's 'no' signal.

After the screening stage, the recruiter wants to present a "short list" of resumes that they can present as a slate of candidates to the client or hiring manager. Some clients are very particular and want the recruiter to "show the work" and as a result the recruiter will share a list of 20 or more candidates. Others are more hands-off and will need only a few candidates in order to make their way through the interview process.

Truly cynical commentators on executive search will tell you that the best executive search firms or consultants try to show the client four candidates. One who's bad is set up as the very first interview, but sets a low bar. The next who is terrific, but too expensive or senior. A third that's just right, but not going to get offered the job or take the job for some reason. And then they show the fourth, who is just as good as the third, but the recruiter feels can be "closed" when an offer is made.

Like I said, it's what the truly cynical will tell you about executive search, and you'll see how that assessment matches up against your own experience.

So for your resume to make it to the slate show to the hiring manager, it needs to show that you have the appetite, the ability, and the ambition to take the role as the next step in your career. And the truth is that, given the volume of resumes a recruiter reviews in his day, all of this takes place in an incredibly short period of time.

To maximize your likelihood of success during those recruiter's seven seconds reviewing your resume, then, is not to have the greatest number of keywords, and not the most far afield buzz phrases, but the most appropriate keywords, terminology, and words that accurately indicate the type of job you'd most like to fill next.

3rd audience: Hiring managers; nobody hires a "VP, Anything"

Sometimes, when asked "what are you looking to do next?", we allow ourselves to slip into a lazy habit that seems harmless but is actually a critical mistake.

While you know that your reply "oh, I'm open to anything" means that you're flexible about your next steps; that you have an attractive humility about your impressive accomplishments and you're not putting on airs; that you're a team player who is committed to the team's goals and targets and mission rather than prioritizing your own; while **you** know that all of these subtle messages are being transmitted when you say "oh, I'm open to anything", your future boss doesn't. Your third, most important, audience, needs you to be specific, spell it out, and sell them on the benefits of what it feels like to be your boss.

Hiring managers, your third audience, are looking to hire someone to fill a specific role on their team to help them achieve their 2019 plan. Remember, their experience is that they are reviewing a couple dozen resumes their recruiter has provided for the open role. If they're hiring for more than one role, or more than one position, that number quickly gets up into the hundreds. Even on our own Ladders system, which screens out most of the inappropriate applications, employers get about 40 resumes on average for each job they promote with us.

So while it is obvious to you that you are being accommodating, it comes across to your future boss like you're being wishy-washy. That you don't have a defined "value add". That you're uncertain of how or where to apply your skills best. That rather than invite you in for the interview, perhaps she ought to look at the next candidate in the pile, who might be a little sharper.

Just as the iPad buyer is looking to do something specific: watch movies, play games, surf the web, or read email, it would be far less compelling to say 'it's an electronics product that can do pretty much anything you want it to.' While that's true, it puts too much of the effort and the guesswork on the user.

Your future boss has a plan they need to deliver in 2019. Present the benefits you can bring, strongly and clearly.

In a world connected by the internet, when information overload is high and the competition so fierce, it is more important than ever to stand for something specific.

Nobody hires a VP, Anything.

4th audience: the world's computers

The toughest audience for your resume is a software called **ATS**, short for "**Applicant Tracking System**". Too often, an ATS mangles all the good work that you've put into a resume. Avoid the worst outcomes by having a straightforward presentation that is heavy on getting the words right, and light on unique, quirky, or idiosyncratic formatting.

When you reflect on the pros and cons of technology in your own field, you'll remember that it's proven to be an amazing tool at connecting us globally, rapidly, with rich data. You'll also be frustrated with how often it sends the wrong thing to the wrong person at the wrong time, or produces an outcome you were totally not expecting.

Same thing goes for the ATS technology at the core of most HR departments today. ATS's are often criticized by HR people for being difficult to work with, and criticized by candidates who often feel lost navigating through them.

Perhaps the best way to think about an ATS and how it processes your resume is to imagine a company's ATS as a precocious teenager assigned to re-type your entire resume into the company's database. The teenager wouldn't understand what any of the words mean, might get things wrong if the structure or formatting is too complex, but would "mostly" be able to re-type accurately what they see on the page.

Therefore, crafting a resume that does not get mangled by an ATS is almost entirely about being defensive -- avoiding practices, features, or formatting that could confuse the ATS / precocious teenager:

- Special characters should be avoided. What's a special character? Anything that's in the 'Special Characters' tab on Microsoft Word, or 'Insert > Special Character' in Google Docs.
- Avoid ● ⇒ Ω ♫ ⌘, emojis, fancy arrows, Greek lettering, musical notation, and abstruse keyboard notations.
- Keep your formatting extraordinarily simple. Tabs are mostly OK so long as you don't overdo it. But tables, sections, and any other word editor feature that adds hidden structure to your resume is bad.
- Please keep it simple with your headings. Your work experience should be called 'Work', or 'Work Experience'. It should not be "Things I Have Excelled and Thrived At In This Life".
- Your educational background should be titled "Education", not "School of Hard Knocks" or "Degrees Received." It's important for the ATS to be able to import this data into the correct sections of the database, and if you use clever or non-standard headings, you may confuse the ATS / precocious teenager.
- Only use the basic or default fonts in Google Docs and Microsoft Word. The precocious teenager might not have the fancier fonts installed on his computer, and will quickly get bored trying to find them.

- Assume the ATS / precocious teenager has a short attention span and will lose all of the fancy formatting, fonts, structure, columns, and aesthetic balance you create in your resume.

In twenty years in the business, I have often heard the media, job candidates or designers gush over a clever resume design. In that same time, I have never (ever) at any professional event, meeting, function, blog, magazine, email, newsletter, or confab, heard a recruiter of HR professional gush about a great resume format. There is simply no advantage, ever, to a candidate having a clever, quirky, differentiated resume format.

So save yourself and the ATS / precocious teenager a lot of grief and keep your resume extraordinarily simple and straightforward. Your time and effort are better spent elsewhere.

Less is more

We all deal with loss in our lives -- in this chapter you're going to deal with loss also -- the loss of past achievements that are very near and dear to your heart, but that don't support your job goals.

We all have them -- me included. As a freshman at Yale, an enterprising group of us living in the same residential college (that's what they call dorms at Yale) put together a proposal to take over the college's coffee shop. The professor assigned to manage the dorm agreed and we giddily took over "The Buttery" and ran it for the next several years. Our enthusiasm was only marginally damaged when we did the math and discovered that we were making less than minimum wage for all the hours we put into it.

Nonetheless, that achievement stayed on my resume for well over a decade because I loved to be reminded of it. "Bright college years" is the old Yale school song, and thinking about my time in college, and the antics we got into, and the friends made there, felt wonderful. Even years later, it was a happy trip down nostalgia lane for me every time I reminded myself of those times by glancing at my resume.

It made me happy to see 'The Buttery' there.

But all of those wonderful feelings didn't justify this achievement taking up 3 lines on my resume in the years ahead. While I thought it showed pluck, and energy, and entrepreneurial zeal, it was largely lost on recruiters, and hiring managers, because absolutely nobody really knows what a "Buttery" is. (Turns out it's a funny old word from Europe related to where the butler stashed his stuff -- Yale had adopted it for some of our coffee shops).

You, too, have achievements from back in the day that don't belong on your resume. They come from a time in college, or at your first job, or even just a really wonderful experience you had in your last position that you are fond of in a way that doesn't reflect the achievement's value in your professional advertisement, but instead reflects the warm fuzzy feeling you get when you think back to that time.

Or perhaps it was an achievement that was hard-fought, that caused you nights and weeks of anxiety, and when the triumph came one misty morning, it smelled like... victory. Sometimes those battles, and conflicts, and times of terrible effort and concentration that go along with huge achievements have a rosy glow in hindsight. When those achievements support your professional advertisement message, they ought to be included.

But when those achievements are simply self congratulatory, represent the joy of victory, or mark a struggle that was more important emotionally than it was professionally, it is important for you to leave them off your resume.

Only the achievements and accomplishments that support your professional message deserve to be included. And every achievement that you select to show on your resume should help deliver the message to your future boss about the benefits you can deliver to them in the coming years.

So you'll need to go through a painful, bittersweet exercise. Review all of your past experiences that you loved -- an internship, a college course, a lifeguard job, an early achievement. If it, in fact, supports a key part of your benefit to your future boss, then definitely keep it on your resume.

But if, as I discovered in the case of my college nighttime snack shop experience, it is on your resume for reasons that are more sentimental than they are practical, you'll need to make the hard choice and remove it.

But don't mourn its departure too wistfully. After some time passes, you'll discover that your enjoyment of the event is just as great with it off your resume. And you'll be even happier with the outcome of having a cleaner, crisper resume that makes the case for your future employment more concisely.

3. Writing the modern resume

What is the floor plan of the modern resume?

Your resume has two pages, 187 square inches, and 25 bullet points to make your case. This floor plan should be well-architected, with everything in its proper place. The good news is that there really is not a lot of room for variation or creativity in these recommendations. Unlike the advice I got from all corners at business school, it is fairly straightforward to craft a correct and easy-to-read resume.

If you have been given quirky, creative, or erroneous advice suggesting that columns, or non-chronological order, or multiple colors, or images, improve a resume, then please discard that advice. For each audience -- the screener, the recruiter, the hiring manager and the back-office computer systems -- unusual or unique features lead to errors in comprehension and review that can only harm your candidacy.

Margins and font size for your resume should not vary from the defaults in your editor. No matter how tempting, delicious, or forbidden the fruit, altering the margins to allow your resume more text is a misunderstanding of how resumes are used by the people who matter. Do not touch that on-screen ruler!

Please stick with the presentation style of a single column of text. More templates are being made with two columns, and the power of a modern writing editor often means that you can achieve a two-column format that does not look obviously wrong. But wrong it is, especially after it is translated from computer to computer to computer.

Resume Length

Professional experience between 10 and 25 years
Your resume will be 2 pages total, composed of a professional summary, a chronological detail of your professional success, an education section followed by awards and inventions, and a brief personal section. You should begin with your contact information at the head of your resume.

Again, here is our format for the two-page resume and links to our online free resources for templates and examples:

www.theladders.com/career-advice/resume-guide
www.theladders.com/free-resume-templates
www.theladders.com/resume-examples

FIRSTNAME I. LASTNAME

firstname.lastname.2019@gmail.com
Address - City - State - Zip Code
(212) 555-1212

GENERAL & OPERATIONS MANAGER

COO • VP, Ops & Admin • Country Manager • Senior Operations Director
Business Development • Revenue Generation • Strategic Planning • Relationship Management
Led Business Growth • Increased Productivity • Reduced Costs • Effective Recruiter
Team Leadership Award 2018 • 3x Executive of the Year • Promoted Early • Public Speaker

WORK EXPERIENCE

Current Company Name, Inc., New York, NY   April 2015 - present
Chief Operating Officer
Leading Contract Manufacturer in Service Industry
- Increased productivity by xx% after taking over supply...
- Delivered 3 new distribution centres on budget...
- Improved results for delivery success goals by xx%...
- Optimized sourcing strategies resulting in 8 new manufacturing...
- Produced savings of $xx million across operations, maintenance...
- Reduced defects by over xx% by implementing large-scale...
- Generated a xx% on-time performance increase by streamlining...
- Exceeded market share goal by x points through reduction of...

Prior Company, Inc., Lake Forest, IL   Jan 2011 - April 2015
General & Operations Manager
$14 Billion Global Manufacturer and Distributor
- Maximized profitability, generating over $xx million annually by implementing...
- Accelerated delivery of new technologies to reduce headcount by 16%, adding...
- Achieved xx days reduction in closing cycle time by overseeing analysis of...
- Sold 3 data centers, generating $xx million in cost reductions...
- Decreased technical and operational costs by xx% by creating strategies...
- Orchestrated xx% revenue growth by developing and executing...
- Streamlined logistics resulting in $xx million in annual cost savings...
- Grew net income by more than xxx% by overseeing...

Middle Company, Inc., City of Industry, CA   2004 - 2011
Promoted early from Product Manager
General & Operations Manager   May 2007 - Jan 2011
- Added 310 basis points to customer satisfaction scores by...
- Gained xx% efficiency improvement by implementing...
- Contributed to a budgetary saving of $xxM through the acquisition...
- Expanded role to supervision of 5 critical distribution locations...

Product Manager   Sep 2004 - May 2007
Operational Product Management
- Awarded patent for osmosis system that reduced costs by 67% in core manufacturing...
- Eliminated 12% of components through product redesign while maintaining quality...
- Introduced a pricing strategy that saw a xx% rise in increased...

First Company, Inc., San Antonio, TX   July 2001 - Sep 2004
Product Manager
Strategic Product Management at Global Industrial Manufacturer
- Saved 23% on operating costs by implementing ordering...
- Minimized customer complaints and increased sales by xx% by restructuring...

EDUCATION
Grad School University Name   2001
Master's in Precisely Specific Degree, Houston, TX
- Winner of award, distinction or honor
- Member of club, society, or organization

Undergraduate College or University Name, Austin, TX   1999
BS/BA in Precisely Specific Degree
- Winner of award, distinction or honor

PERSONAL, PATENTS, AWARDS, TECHNOLOGIES, KEYWORDS (OPTIONAL)

Team Leadership Award 2018, Certified Manager (CM), Conflict Management Certified (CCM), 3x
Employee of the Year (2018, 2016, 2014), Process Improvement Category 2015, JustFood ERP,
NetSuite, Prodsmart, IQMS ERP Software, Integrify, Deskera ERP Software, Risk Mitigation,
Research & Development, Profit & Loss, Lean Manufacturing, JIT, TQM, Purchasing & Supply
Chain Management, Change Agent, Production Cultivation, Production Harvest, XtraCHEF, Parsley,
FiiX, ProLease Maintenance, SiteDocs

Firstname I. Lastname

Professional experience less than 10 years

If you have less than 10 years experience, one page is often the right length for your resume. Your professional summary, if it appears, will only be a single line, and is more likely a normally capitalized sentence. If you graduated less than five years ago, your education may still appear at the top of your resume, depending on whether you are looking for an entry-level or mid-level role.

As you approach 10 years experience, how do you know when expanding to two pages is the right length for your resume? The answer is that when your most recent job is very different in role, responsibility, or expectations from your earliest job, you should expand to two pages. If you've progressed from individual contributor to manager is one example. Or if you've gone from individual contributor at an individual level on a team, to having some policy, architecture, direction, or 'lead' designation, is another.

Professional experience over 25 years
If you have over 25 years experience, you may consider three pages, though two are often sufficient. Follow guidance from recruiters in your specific industry.

If you're at the executive level with 25 total years experience, a third party should be crafting your resume for you. As you know, it's foolish to splurge on the product and skimp on the ad expense, especially if you are the product.

Conversely, if you've been in the same role with the same title for 35 years, then it is appropriate to stick with the one page length. If you've remained an insurance adjuster, or senior accountant, or sales representative, for a decade or more, it is best to stay at one page. Your goal is to accurately signal your job expectations. If you desire to remain at an individual contributor level, you are doing yourself a disservice by sending an inaccurate signal to future employers with a two-page resume.

Resume Structure

Contact information
At the top of the first page, centered, are your name, phone number, tasteful and professional email address, and any social links that you choose to include. Your home address ought to go here, and there's no good reason to exclude it. If you've moved cities in the past ten years, it is **better** to include your home address in the city you desire to work. Overall, however, we do see that home address is increasingly being dropped from resumes by younger professionals without negative impact.

Professional Summary
Your professional summary is three or four lines of text immediately below your contact information that makes your case boldly, optimistically, and projects into the future a bit. This section also highlights past accomplishments and skills deployed.

Reverse-chronologically ordered job history

The jobs you have had over the past fifteen years appear on your resume in reverse chronological order, and cover roughly 25 bullet points. Reverse chronological simply means the most recent experiences are at the top of your resume, the ones furthest in the past at the end of your resume.

The last two years, since 2017, get 4 - 8 bullet points. The work you did 15 years ago, might only get one-half of a line.

Some may suggest that a functionally-ordered or a skills-based resume are acceptable. In American business in 2019, they are not. Stick with reverse chronological order.

Education
Your educational background, again in reverse chronological order, appears after work history. To the extent possible, your education should be recast to support your current professional goals by emphasizing the degrees, clubs, or activities most relevant to your professional career.

Those who are less than five years out of grad school, business school, law school, **may** consider placing their

References Available Upon Request
While this was common until the 2000s, it is no longer considered required or desirable. In 2019, you should leave the mention of 'References available upon request' off your resume entirely.

Start a new resume in a new document

You've created so many memos, slide shows, and spreadsheets over your career that of course it feels like old hat. And you might be tempted to get started on your resume without giving it a second thought. But there are a number of small goofs you could make without knowing it, because of the way modern corporations collect, review, store and manage resumes.

First, always start by creating your brand new resume in a brand new document. You may want to start with a copy and paste, or just pick up with importing your last resume from a prior format. But you don't want to do this because you could be importing bad practices into your new resume.

Your resume's journey is going to take it through the computers, desktops, storage systems, and Applicant Tracking Systems of an untold number of managers, recruiters and corporations. You should not be confident, **at all**, that you understand all the configurations, oddities, flavors, and settings of all those varied environments. I've been doing this twenty years and I'm still continually surprised by the unexpected, and sometimes very bad, systems that HR departments and hiring managers use to assess and review your resume.

By starting in a fresh new document you avoid importing any bad formatting -- odd margins, quirky table structures, unknown or outdated fonts, weird footers and headers -- that may be present in your old resume or in the template you're importing. The formatting quirks can be deadly to your resume's legibility. In some cases, a table that looks great in one format can inadvertently render all the text contained in the table completely invisible on the screens of recruiters.

While it may seem like a shortcut to take your friend's resume and formatting and just change all the words, please do not. You don't know how many hidden formatting errors lurk in the document. You don't know what your friend did or did not get right in using the editor they created it in. And perhaps your friend didn't even create it but imported it herself from yet another friend! All of these unknowns make it not worth risking the legibility and readability of your resume.

Do not copy and paste formatting for the same reasons. Even when you see something terrific, and you want to borrow it for your resume, it's never advisable to copy and paste text with unknown formatting in the background or hidden deep behind the visible text. Always start your resume document from a clean new document.

Do use an editor with which you are familiar. Microsoft Word and Google Docs are the overwhelming choices of Ladders members, and the US professional population generally. If you have a good reason to use something else, please make sure it is a very good reason.

The name of your document should be "Lastname.Firstname.Year.docx" (or .pdf):

Smith.Adam.2019.pdf

If it's past September, start using the next year:

Smith.Adam.2020.pdf

You're probably going to be using this same resume into the New Year anyway and starting early makes you seem ahead of the times. And everybody wants to hire somebody from the future, right?

You may be tempted to rename your resume for each company you send the resume to:

"TwitterResume.pdf"

Please do not. The folks at the company you're sending the resume to know the name of their own company, so what's important to them is your name, not theirs.

Please also do not use your initials ("mc_resume.doc"), your first name only ("marc_resume.doc"), simply the date ("12.2019_resume.doc"), or the word 'final', because it is inevitably followed by the next version ("marc_resume_FINAL_v3.doc"). You're allowed to laugh at that last one because you know it's true.

A clean, new resume, in a clean new document, titled with your last name first, then your given name, followed by the year, is the best practice.

What email address should you use professionally?

If you're using AOL, or your local cable provider, you could be inadvertently shooting yourself in the foot.

Only 1% of new users at Ladders signed up with AOL email addresses in January 2019. And just 5% use Hotmail.com. If you're still using AOL or Hotmail to represent yourself professionally, it could be sending a signal that you're uncomfortable with new technology and that you haven't prioritized keeping your skills up-to-date.

Using your local cable provider's default email -- whether it's bellsouth.net, optonline.net, or tampabay.rr.com -- increases the chances of a typo, leading to a missed connection. Because people don't pay as much attention to what they're typing after the '@' sign, using less-familiar domains in your email should be avoided.

Over 65% of new users at Ladders in January 2019 used **gmail.com**. Because gmail is well-known for its utility, ease-of-use, and power, using gmail as your address is a smart move that also sends the message that you're in step with the times.

Here's a close-up of the typical contact information section on our suggested resume:

What's before the '@' sign is important too.

Common 'household' or 'joint' email strategies such as 'jimandnancy@', 'smithhousehold@', or 'bluthfamily@' are not good email addresses to use for your professional life.

Professionals are accustomed to writing directly to other professionals. Requesting that they email your spouse & kids when contacting you is awkward.

As with naming your resume file, the best email address is your first name, followed by a dot, followed by your last name, at gmail.com:

sheldon.cooper@gmail.com

If that's taken, then for the purposes of your job search, add **next** year's number to your address:

sheldon.cooper.2020@gmail.com

Keep the contact information section as compact as possible. With plenty of ways for you to be contacted, you'd prefer to include only the most important and then utilize the rest of the space on your resume for advertising your abilities.

Centered text, with your name in larger font, in bold, on the first line, is standard. Any other flashiness is unhelpful and unwelcome.

Social media on your resume and on the web

Facebook is rarely included on resumes. Remember to review what's available about you publicly on Facebook, because your future employer will be visiting your profile. If it's strictly a personal account, it's best to lock it down, and not make it publicly available at all.

Instagram is for fields where a visual presence or sense of style are important. In 2019, an Instagram account on your resume is increasingly welcome. There's a growing sense that Instagram is supplanting Snapchat for ephemeral photos and Stories. Instagram also seems to be gaining a reputation as a more positive place than its corporate parent Facebook.

For LinkedIn, opinions vary as to whether InMail is a blessing or a curse. Make your decision and include your LinkedIn link accordingly.

Twitter was once a great destination for the latest snippet-sized thinking from everyone in the world. By 2019, enough leading lights have publicly renounced Twitter, relapsed, and re-renounced that it's worth considering whether you provide yours publicly. For years, I included @cenedella on my public materials, but in 2019, I no longer do so.

With regard to dating services, please make sure you're comfortable with whatever material you have made available on dating services such as Tinder, Bumble, Match and others. Especially those that show up in Google searches of you. You may want to comprehensively review your settings to ensure that your profiles are private or confidential enough that it's not an issue.

For all internet sites and networks, material that is not strictly professional should be behind a privacy, pay, or confidentiality wall.

The professional summary is the most effective way to deliver your message

In your professional summary, you will make your most effective, most concise, most powerful pitch for the job you want. Using short words and brief phrases, this section stands out from the rest of your resume in a dramatic and compelling way. We will use that power to convey precisely the message we want your professional ad to deliver. While it represents only 1/10th of the space on your resume, the professional summary should be where you spend ⅓ or more of your time.

Your professional summary begins with a three or four word professional description of who you are. You'll want to include only the three or four words that capture the essence of your professional career at this point. Our example here is a **General & Operations Manager**, but you may be an **Innovative Financial Executive**, a **Senior Leader in CPG Marketing**, a **Gaming Technology CTO**, an **Accomplished VP Enterprise Sales**, or a **Leading Biotech Research Scientist**.

Whichever it is, this bold, ALL CAPS, description of your professional standing at the top of your resume is your calling card, your summary, and the marketing pitch for your candidacy. It's worth spending several hours getting this exactly right.

After this professional description, your professional summary is another three or four lines long. Each line is a list of words or phrases that, in combination, support the compelling picture of the professional description above, and the role you'd like next. The jobs or roles you are seeking should flow logically from the achievements, capabilities, and characteristics you display here.

You'll spend as much time on what to leave out, as what to include. Miles Davis said "Music is the space between the notes. It's not the notes you play; it's the notes you don't play." For you, it's the words and achievements and titles that you leave out that reinforce for your audience who you are and what you'll do next.

In total, your professional summary will include 12 to 16 phrases spread across three to four lines. The first of the four lines is a list of **job titles** you want. The next line is a list of **professional skills** you have. The third is a list of **achievement categories** that you excel in. The **optional** fourth line is a further illumination of skills or achievements or a more explicit indication of the kind of company, role or industry you're targeting.

This specific ordering suggests a pattern to follow. If it makes more sense to you to change the order or the themes, you have the flexibility to do that. So while it makes more sense to group skills on one line and achievements on another, if the specific order of job title - skills - achievements - awards does not work for your situation, you should change it as you see fit, and as reads best for you.

The professional summary encapsulates your first impression to your four audiences. Like all first impressions, it is important and can be defining. The same resume with the same accomplishments reads very differently with these anodyne, generic terms "Seasoned Executive - Manager - P&L Responsibility - Industry Expert" versus the more direct and specific "COO - SVP, Operations - Turn-around Expert - Delivered $2 bn Shareholder Value".

Again, while it might seem obvious to you what someone like you would want to do next, for your four audiences, it's not. After all, it's what you want to do, and with all the various paths open to professionals, it is very difficult for someone outside of yourself to know what you're thinking about doing for your next gig.

In fact, given how different people are, you can be assured that someone just like you spoke to the recruiter, or screener, or hiring manager last month, last week, or even yesterday, and despite having the precise background that you have, that person told them of a completely different career plan. I've seen it enough to know that I can never guess -- in fact, that's exactly why one of the first things I ask in hiring is "so what are you looking to do next?"

You'd be surprised at the answers!

In our example here, we've clarified that our resume is for a **General & Operations Manager**, who is looking for roles with the title COO, VP, Operations and Administration, Country Manager, and so forth. Listing those titles specifically make it easy for Audience #1, the screener, to understand which roles to select you for. It makes it easy for Audience #2, the recruiting professional, to understand that you're looking to continue your successful trajectory in your field. It makes it easy for Audience #3, your future boss, to know who you are and where you're headed. And it makes easy for Audience #4, the ATS, to understand what titles to associate your candidacy with.

As always on resumes, the more specific you can be, the better. Your four audiences must come away with an explicit understanding of the type of job in which you're interested in, the titles they should consider you for, and the types of activities at which you excel and your key capabilities.

Formatting considerations for this section are to ensure that you keep the descriptive lines to four lines only. Don't go over the line ends and cause gaps in spacing as the software tries to deal with a word or two extra on the next line. And keep the entire section centered.

Job titles

On the first line, you'll list 3 to 5 job titles of jobs you would actually accept as your next job. It's important to note that these are the titles of the job you want **next**, not of the jobs you have had in the past, or the job you currently have. You should think of this line as a "role wanted" advertisement -- the place in your professional ad where you inform recruiters and hiring managers of the job you desire, and believe you're a good fit for. This first line of your professional summary is the most effective area of your resume for communicating your expectations, so you should use it to do so. Merely repeating the job titles that you will be listing in your chronological history is a wasted opportunity -- you don't need to advertise for the jobs you're leaving!

Now it's important to note that it does not matter that you have never actually had this job title in the past, but it ought to be a plausible next step in your professional career. Rather, you're advertising your ambition to the screener, the recruiter, or hiring manager looking to hire someone for that particular role and title.

Calibrating precisely the title you're looking for is easier, of course, if you plan on staying in a similar-sized company. A VP, Marketing at one tiny startup can plausibly lay claim to the ability to fulfill the VP, Marketing role at another tiny startup. And a Finance Manager at one Fortune 1000 company is well within her rights to indicate that Senior Manager, Finance is her target for her next gig. Complications arise when you're considering all company sizes -- having been a CMO at three different five-person start-ups does not make it at all likely that you'd be considered for a role with a lower level, such as Director or VP, at a Fortune 500 company.

Because there are no hard and fast rules that make it easy, you'll need to use your business judgment to determine what qualifies as a suitable title for which you ought to be considered.

Examples of the first line of your professional summary are:

VP, Marketing • Director, Marketing • Brand Marketing Leader • CMO

or

Sales Representative | Business Development Executive | Account Executive or

Logistics Manager * Logistics Senior Manager * Operations
Manager * Plant Supervisor

or

Financial Director - Director, FP&A - Credit Analyst -
Director, Planning

You'll notice the separators can be anything tasteful and
understated -- an asterisk, a dot, a vertical bar or a hyphen.

Having typed out your future job titles, you may perhaps
come to a crossroads where you ask yourself: "Isn't a
resume a strictly historical document? If I put a title on my
resume that I haven't had yet, is that lying or fabrication?"

These are valid questions, so let's review them.

A resume is a **marketing** document. It is not a transcript, a
work history, or a sworn affidavit claiming to represent your
past in precisely legal terms. It is a marketing document,
and you are marketing your skills, capabilities and objectives
in a positive light in order to communicate a message to
future employers regarding the next role for which you'd like
to be considered.

While it would not be truthful to indicate that you possessed
a specific title, during a specific historical time period, at a
specific company, in the past, if you did not in fact have that

title and role, it **is** truthful to indicate that your own professional assessment is that you are now at the professional level where the titles you have indicated are appropriate for your skill set and experience. Someone else may quibble as to whether or not you're ready to make that step, but your professional summary is a mere advertisement that you are ready for the role.

We are seeing this more and more widely in common practice throughout the millions of resumes at Ladders each year; it is the sensible distinction between a marketing document (your resume) and a factual transcription (your employment history record). I think the Baby Boomers inherited from their parents and generations past an understanding of the resume as a summary, rather than a sales document, leading them to feel that resumes must be transcripts. Modern practice has varied considerably towards them being advertisements, and that is the strong advice of this book and this author.

To recap, it's fine to advertise your enthusiasm and ambition for specific roles, but not acceptable to have outright falsehoods or claim accomplishments that are objectively not true.

Professional skills

The second line of your professional summary focuses on professional skills -- your skills and capabilities that are important to your success in the job titles laid out above.

These should be skills that you **currently** possess and should be "level appropriate".

Because this is an advertisement, you want to showcase those skills that are most relevant to your next professional step up. Understanding what your future boss will be looking for, you should highlight skills that are most clearly relevant to the types of achievements or accomplishments he will be looking for from this role.

Please consider that at your next job, the skills you are currently using will be one notch less relevant. The basic skills for the role will not be relevant at all. The advanced skills at your current job will be the basic, expected skills in your next role. And the skills you are currently stretching yourself to acquire -- those that are currently at the very fingertips of your reach -- will be the ones that you'll be expected to develop and put into practice day after day.

So if you're currently an individual contributor and want to move up to a team lead, or a senior individual contributor role, rather than highlight skills related to your individual practice, you want to call out those skills that show the elements of team leadership and accountability.

And if you're a manager looking to step up and become a manager of managers, you'll focus on your ability to manage output, process, accountability, and communication, more than your ability to manage individual team members, the work output, and team member level tasks and productivity.

Do not list skills that are obvious or would be assumed for someone at your level. For example, if you're applying for C-suite jobs, listing "time management" or "presentation skills" would be far too junior to mention in your summary.

Examples for the second line could include:

Agile Development • Software Architecture • Engineer Recruiting • Technology Innovation

or

Payroll & Benefits | Employee Training & Development | Culture | Employee Relations

or

Litigation * Corporate Counsel * Contracts Negotiation * Risk Mitigation

or

Cost Containment - Project Leadership - General Contracting - Government Relations

Past achievements

On the third line of your professional summary, you will list 3 to 5 phrases that describe your demonstrated past success. Any type of achievements or attributes for which you have received recognition are appropriate, and those that best demonstrate your mastery of your prior roles are best.

In the chronological section ahead, you'll specify those achievements in detail, so perhaps the best approach will be to revisit this section after you've completed your work history chronology. Summarizing the three to five **most important** achievements provides you the best opportunity to make a concise case for why past success is indicative of future results.

Examples:

President's Club • Top-producing Saleswoman • Exceeds Quota • Consultative Selling Expert

or

Launched New Brands | Clio Award-Winning Campaigns | Increased Efficiency

or

Increased Team Velocity * Shipped New Products * Excellent Recruiter * AWS Migration

or

FDA Review Expert - Acquisition Identification - Received 17 Patents

Situational, recognition or industry considerations

On the optional fourth line, you can include additional skills, capabilities and achievements, and also provide additional color around the types of situations you are looking for; internal, external, or industry awards and recognition, or indications of industry interest that may not be clear from other items in your professional summary.

Examples might include "Marketer of the Year 2018", "Turnaround Expert", "Growth Company Executive", "Successful Public Speaker", "Startup Leader", "CPG Veteran", or "Airline Expert."

Your optional fourth line is a great place to add additional flavor to your overall initial presentation, and round out the picture of who you'd like to be next.

To repeat, there's no penalty for mixing and matching the themes on these various lines, but there's no benefit either. Save yourself the time and aggravation by keeping it simple and following this outline.

The chronological detail of your professional success

The bulk of a resume is made up of the chronological detail of your professional success, starting with your most recent job first. This is your chance to **detail** your successes and achievements, not simply list past job titles and duties, or provide an inventory of staff composition and budget size. The purpose of your chronological history is to display for your future boss the types of benefits past bosses have garnered from having the good sense to hire you.

For each job you've had, you'll have an entry including the company name, title, description and dates.

Company name

Company name seems straightforward and typically is. There is some variation today in whether to use the company's formal name with the appropriate qualifier -- Incorporated, Company -- and whether to use the abbreviation or not. As there is no standard rule, use the formal company name in industries with a tendency towards formality, and the more casual version in casual industries.

I'd be inclined to call it "Pillsbury Winthrop Shaw Pittman LLP", not "Pillsbury", in the legal field, at the same time I'd recommend "Google" and not "Alphabet, Inc." if you're a mid-level manager in the internet industry.

Whichever way you choose, stay consistent throughout your resume in how you treat company names.

In the case of mergers & acquisitions, bankruptcies, or name changes that occurred after your departure, there is, again, no hard and fast rule. Use whatever feels most effective from a marketing standpoint. In my own case, I worked at HotJobs.com from 2000 to 2002, when I helped sell it to Yahoo! for a half-billion dollars. Over the past 16 years, it has appeared on my resume in various forms:

Hotjobs.com, Ltd. (NASD: HOTJ), and then...
Hotjobs.com, a Yahoo! Company, and then...
Hotjobs *(after it was sold to Monster by Yahoo!)*, and then back to...
Hotjobs.com (NASD: HOTJ), when it was closed down by Monster, and I wanted to highlight my role at a public company 16 years ago.

There's no set answer for how to handle company names through these transitions, little in the way of negative judgments regarding the choice you make, and relatively low stakes involved, so your choice, as long as it is consistent, should be based on what helps tell your story most effectively.

In the unfortunate cases where your company was involved in a notorious scandal -- Bernard L. Madoff Securities, Enron, Global Crossing, CountryWide Financial -- there's little you can do other than list the company accurately and address the subject head on either in your achievements "Survived corporate scandal impacting a separate division -- no person in our group was accused of or found to have been involved in unethical behavior", in person or on the phone with the recruiter. Some have reported success in handling the matter head-on in the company description "Worked in separate entity from the infamous investment management business" or "Blind-sided professional at disgraced energy trading company."

It's worth remembering that some employers do, in fact, appreciate the type of grit and determination that goes along with overcoming this kind of adversity. Should you find yourself in this unfortunate situation, do not presume that everybody is snickering -- some may be more intrigued than put off.

Titles and employment dates

Now's the time to be precise. You're dealing with history, here, not with ambition or dreams, and history is all about facts. You'll list your actual title, as it appeared in your offer letter or subsequent company correspondence. It is quite important to be precise, as you are representing that you held this title at this company at this time. Small inflations can come back to bite you -- promoting yourself to manager or director of a team when you were in fact a step or half-step lower. Among the few things that companies have been known to check during background checks are titles, so it is both ethically and procedurally necessary to ensure that your resume matches the company's records precisely.

The common practice has remained to include both month and year in the date. Despite my long-time advocacy for simplifying these dates to year only -- there's really not a lot of additional information conveyed by the month -- you should continue to follow the common practice, writing January 2017 - December 2019, for example. I'll continue my advocacy for simplifying and let you know next year if I've made progress.

Multiple jobs and promotions at one company require careful presentation, both for the understanding of the people who will read your resume, as well as the systems and automated computer parsers that will translate your resume from a document into a storable version in the company's systems.

In the case of multiple jobs consecutively at the same company, the best approach is to put the years served inclusive next to the company name, and then the actual stretch in each role, as expressed by month-date - month-date, next to each position title.

Company or role description

Increasingly popular in recent years is the trend towards describing the company and or the responsibilities of the role in a line underneath the company name. This succinct summary of important background information is quite an effective way to convey the facts about your role or the company. In fact, matters such as staff size, budget and hiring circumstances are best dealt with on this line.

For example, you might write any of the following as a description of the employer:
"A global water transport company"
"A national fast food chain"
"A leading professional services firm", or
"A Fortune 50 diversified industrial company"

You may also choose to address your staffing or responsibility:
"Responsible for Western Region Sales at regional machine tools manufacturer"
"Managed $30 mm ad budget for national hotel chain"
"Held P&L responsibility for $310 mm engine division"

Or the circumstances that led you to the role:
"Recruited by CEO to take over all HR operations nationally"
"Promoted multiple times over decade at this leading software integration firm"
"Selected to lead post-merger leading CPG firm by combined Board"

As a means of concisely communicating the size, shape, or circumstances of your role or employer, using this descriptive line is an excellent means. While not required, it can greatly help you increase the amount of information you get across without taking up more valuable bullet points.

Handling gaps -- sired, fired, retired

Handling gaps in your employment history is distressing for any professional. I'm being a bit tongue in cheek when describing this as sired, fired, or retired, but those are the most common gap causes.

Sired. You or your spouse gave birth and you decided to stay at home for some number of years. That time period is up and you're looking to get back into the workplace.

Fired. You picked the wrong job, wrong boss, wrong industry, or the wrong one was thrust upon you, and you ended up being shown the door. Landing the next role has not happened as quickly as you would've liked and you have a gap longer than 12 months to explain.

Retired. You had decided to downshift and seek out the finer things in life, you've taken a gap year, or simply travelled for a year or two because circumstances afforded you the opportunity. But now it's time to get back to having a work family, or a paycheck, or a career.

In each of these cases, it's always better if you've had a plausible institutional connection during the gap period. Non-profit work is the obvious best and easiest one. Consulting roles, even at your own firm, count. Paid work done on a project basis for friends or former colleagues can also fit the bill. Any of these is better than a final date on your most recent employment that is 12+ months in the past.

But in the case where that just wasn't the situation -- you've been the stay-at-home parent for the past seven years, as an example -- your goal is to minimize the amount of advertising space you spend describing what is not, after all, your most effective selling point. Ideally, you encapsulate it in one optimistic, forward-looking, positive line of text:

Stay-at-home parent for family of four, energized to return to work. 2011- 2019

Or to cover a time of travel:

Fortunate to travel 13 countries before returning to focus on professional career. 2015 - 2019

Or the unenviable, unwanted, employment gap:

Returning to work after a period of personal exploration and growth.   2016 - 2019

In all of these cases, your best approach to managing a period of time when you were not progressing your career professionally is the same -- positive, brief, crisp, succinct -- and then move on to parts of your professional ad that do beneficially reflect your professional capabilities. After all, the iPad ad does not dwell on the fact that it does not have a built-in keyboard. Non-selling points should be navigated around rather than allowed to inhabit too much real estate on your resume.

You've got 25 bullets

For a typical experienced professional with more than ten years experience, you'll have twenty-five bullet points across two pages to make your case. If you're earlier in your career, you may have only 10-15 bullet points across one page. In either case, those bullet points are scarce, precious, and valuable. Each is a careful investment.

You'll remember that "your resume is a professional advertisement, targeted toward your future boss, with the goal of landing an interview for a job that you can succeed in." Bullets are where you entice potential interviewers by providing **quantified, proven results** that detail your successes. Each bullet is constructed of a **success verb** and a **specific numerical accomplishment** in your field or role.

Allocate bullets according to the job's importance in landing your next gig. In general, the most recent year or two will loom largest. Thus, the last five years get 10 to 15 bullets. The next five get 5 to 10. The next five get 5 in total. Anything beyond 15 years ago gets zero bullets -- as difficult as it might be to let go, the sentence that begins with "One of the reasons to hire me is the experience I had in 2002 with..." is simply not persuasive to bosses looking to hire in 2019.

As you're writing each bullet point, craft it to persuade an employer to hire you because of the benefits you can deliver.

In *Ladders 2019 Interviews Guide* you'll ask potential employers and recruiters to tell you the three key things they're looking for in a role they are hiring. This is a terrific way to stand out as most candidates don't ask, even though hiring managers and HR people are only too happy to give specifics. You're making their job easier.

In crafting these bullet points, you might also practice reading out loud the phrase "You should hire me in 2019 for this role because I…" followed by the text of each bullet. Bullets are written to support your argument that you can bring benefits to your hiring manager right now, in this year.

Show, don't tell. Within the confines of confidentiality, bullets should provide specific proof to support the skills and accomplishments you've claimed in your Professional Summary. Simply asserting you're good at this or capable at that isn't persuasive. For each bullet, describe the accomplishment with specific details. It is those specific results, specific stories and specific successes that resonate most with future bosses.

Grew, increased, augmented: making good verb choices without a thesaurus

The structure for each of your bullet points is a **success verb** plus **specific numerical data** regarding an accomplishment in your field or role. Which means that you're in the market for 25 or so verbs.

Finding enough different verbs to say "I did it" in a clever way is often a struggle for professionals writing their resumes. Typical resume advice has focused on making sure that each verb is an active verb, but we've found two problems with this advice.

First, most Americans don't work with active vs. passive verbs on a daily basis, so the concept is not entirely relevant to their lives. "Was shot out of a cannon", for example, doesn't count.

And second, even the stable of active verbs includes some very bland duds that do nothing to help persuade a future employer. My least favorite active verb is 'managed', but there are others equally as tepid such as 'established', 'defined', and 'performed'. None of these are very good, even though they are active, because they don't sell your future employer on what you are able to do, or what benefits you are able to bring to their team. After all, white-collar employees by definition establish, manage, define and perform a wide variety of tasks. But were you any good at them? That's the important fact a hiring manager or recruiter wants to know.

Which makes it important that every bullet point in your resume include a **success verb**, not just an active verb. Success verbs demonstrate success - because you were there, something got better, something improved, something progressed. Verbs such as increased, decreased, improved, reduced, are all success verbs.

Explicitly forbidden are active verbs and phrases that are nonetheless static: "managed", "my responsibilities included", "hired to...", "was responsible for" and so forth. Verbs that merely tell a fact rather than show you in a heroic light.

Rather than leave you wondering what success verbs might be, I'm providing you a precise list of 25 success verbs you can use for the twenty-five bullets on your resume. Simplest would be to use these, **and only these**, verbs. Unless you have a good reason to expand your variety, the below success verbs can cover most bullets you can think of. Limiting your choices will save plenty of time and headache while ensuring a higher quality resume.

This might seem boring, but unless you are applying to be a thesaurus writer, **none of your four audiences care how clever your success verbs are**. The millions of hours lost each year to professionals like you looking up synonyms for "improved" is a complete waste of time.

List of Success Verbs
Accelerated
Achieved
Added
Awarded
Contributed
Decreased
Delivered
Eliminated
Exceeded
Expanded
Gained
Generated
Grew
Improved
Increased
Introduced
Maximized
Minimized
Optimized
Orchestrated
Produced
Reduced
Saved
Sold
Streamlined

WORK EXPERIENCE

Current Company Name, Inc., New York, NY   April 2015 - present
Chief Operating Officer
Leading Contract Manufacturer in Service Industry
- Increased productivity by xx% after taking over supply...
- Delivered 3 new distribution centres on budget...
- Improved results for delivery success goals by xx%...
- Optimized sourcing strategies resulting in 8 new manufacturing...
- Produced savings of $xx million across operations, maintenance...
- Reduced defects by over xx% by implementing large-scale...
- Generated a xx% on-time performance increase by streamlining...
- Exceeded market share goal by x points through reduction of...

Prior Company, Inc., Lake Forest, IL   Jan 2011 - April 2015
General & Operations Manager
$14 Billion Global Manufacturer and Distributor

In our example above of a resume experience, we've stuck to precisely eight of the verbs from the success verbs list. Spread across the two pages of a resume, these twenty-five verbs won't repeat, they'll convey action, and they'll serve to jog your memory about those things you did that were **successful** - when you increased, delivered, improved, or optimized your company's business.

On the other hand, a great example of how stating the obvious in your bullet points can set you back is the classic filler "Hired to be Vice President, Western Region". Look, we live in the United States of America in the 21st century. **Of course** you were **hired** for your current role! I wasn't assuming that you had inherited it from your father, the Duke of Sales, Western Region. This isn't the Game of Thrones, we both know. So why are your wasting valuable space in your resume telling your audience something they already know based on your title?

And given the nature of the modern organization, if you're a manager, **of course** you've managed some number of fellow human beings. And **of course** you were given a budget with which to do something interesting with those human beings in the service of the organization's greater goals.

So when you begin a bullet point with empty non-achievements such as "I was hired, I managed and I was responsible for..." you are squandering the opportunity to showcase the benefits you brought to your boss and your company in your prior role.

Of course, it's not enough to just have the verb, you need a specific numerical accomplishment, too.

Double the number of numbers on your resume

I have never seen a resume with too many numbers!

A good rule of thumb is to count the dollar signs $, percentages %, and specific numbers 123567890, on your resume, and then **double** them.

Quantifying your success with specific numerical data is extraordinarily helpful to your goal of getting called back for the interview. It makes it easier for the screener to understand that you actually did something. It makes it easier for the recruiter to sell your story to the hiring manager when you give them more raw material to work with. And it makes it easier for your future boss to daydream your past performance into next year's budget.

Product Manager   Sep 2004 - May 2007
Operational Product Management
- Awarded patent for osmosis system that reduced costs by 67% in core manufacturing...
- Eliminated 12% of components through product redesign while maintaining quality...
- Introduced a pricing strategy that saw a xx% rise in increased...

First Company, Inc., San Antonio, TX   July 2001 - Sep 2004
Product Manager
Strategic Product Management at Global Industrial Manufacturer
- Saved 23% on operating costs by implementing ordering...
- Minimized customer complaints and increased sales by xx% by restructuring...

EDUCATION
Grad School University Name   2001

For each bullet point, after the success verb comes a **number** expressed in dollars, percentages, or a simple, straight-up, "plain old" number.

Your most recent job, with 10 bullet points might read like this:
- Increased x by %
- Decreased x by %
- Improved x by $
- Reduced x by $
- Introduced new x that led to # more....
- Eliminated old x that led to # less...
- Successfully added # new x....
- Achieved the removal of # new x...
- Maximized x through y
- Minimized x through y

In our resume example above, we've taken the early jobs and shown how even those first jobs out of school can be quantified. Your employer had you there for a year, two, or more -- what was better about the company because you were there? Quantifying it brings your performance to life and is more persuasive than a vague statement that you improved things qualitatively.

As shown in the example, the "x" can be profits, costs, clients, vendors, products, practice areas, strategies, risk, volatility, and any other metric in your professional endeavor that has relevance to your success and skill in your role. You'll be surprised at how many you can write using this template, and, again, how this process jogs your memory for all the great stuff you've done...

- Increased new customer visits by 17% without increasing ad budget.
- Decreased AWS bill by 42% through improved architecture (vs. 19% industry average)
- Improved revenue per SaaS client by $4,250 through consultative sales training.
- Reduced cost-per-hire by $7,010 through employee referral program.
- Introduced 2 new products that led to 2,500,000 increase in MAUs.
- Eliminated old systems that led to a 75 FTE reduction in offshore headcount.
- Successfully added 3 productive warehouses to our nationwide network.
- Achieved the removal of 5,000 external firm billable hours per year by reorganizing internal staffing.
- Maximized productivity growth through 15% improvement in cycle time.
- Minimized capital expenditures through 12% decrease in downtime.

For variety's sake, the 25 success verbs on our list offer a unique construction for each of your resume's twenty-five bullet points. If you wanted, you could pick five and simply repeat them five times each. No recruiter, no hiring manager, cares about the variety of synonyms used on your resume. It's far better to keep it simple and focus your time resources on other areas of your resume.

Quantities are more persuasive

Because I have never seen a resume with too many numbers, ideally, you'll have a number in every single bullet point. Being specific only helps your persuasive case by enumerating your success at every step along the path.

But, you might say, I brought amazing non-quantified value to the organization! I introduced Agile Development, led a huge bond offering, brought innovative logistics strategies to bear, or reorganized our selling methodology.

Yes. I agree those are impressive and important achievements.

But they are only impressive and important to the extent they are quantifiable. New methodologies, exhibiting leadership, or bringing innovation to a company are interesting to your bosses' bosses only to the extent they improve, **quantifiably**, the outcome of the company -- more users, more revenue, faster turnaround, higher client satisfaction, fewer costs, greater profitability.

Your bosses are judged, ultimately, on the quantities they produce. The better you align yourself, and show that you are able to contribute to their achieving those goals, the more likely they are to see you as a solution to their problems today.

In addition, the harder it is for you to think of a way to quantify your results, the more impact actually doing so will have. If you're in a role that you're finding difficult to express quantifiably, isn't every other candidate also having trouble doing the same?

And if they're all having the same problem, how much **more** would someone who **did** quantify their results stand out? A lot?

A compliance professional in the finance industry -- someone whose job is to keep his finance colleagues out of legal and regulatory trouble -- asked me about this last year. "Compliance", as it is actually practiced, is not an overly numerical field. Internal reporting in compliance departments doesn't support a quantified approach. Management and reward structures don't either. And the finance professionals upon whom compliance is being practiced don't communicate with their compliance colleagues in a quantifiable way except to grouse "well, there's another deal you lost me!"

So while acknowledging that compliance is not a field in which quantifiable results play a large part, my query back to him was "well, how much **more** would you stand out with your resume, and in interviews, if you did show the finance professionals in the business that you cared about numbers?

They talk about their **own** performance in terms of numbers all the time, don't they? And don't they sometimes express frustration when colleagues don't understand how strongly numbers drive their own professional experience? If your resume indicated 'supported a growing team of 327 finance professionals in closing 714 opportunities, while preventing 24 non-compliant deals, in 2018, and assisted in generating a 24% increase over the prior year, to $565 mm in revenue', how much **more** would you stand out among all the applicants? And how strongly might the finance professionals advocate for your hire?"

Over the years, I've had professionals from a wide variety of fields adamantly tell me their role could not possibly be numerically described: talent bookers for conferences (really? Signed 12% more talent for the year, generating 15% increase in attendance at our shows and and 0.1 point improvement in our NPS score), managers of grounds crews (really? Reduced budget 3% while maintaining high standards at 37 amusement parks while limiting the increase in complaints to under 1% for the year), auditors (really? Reduced rework on audit by 5% in second year through better planning and asset allocation while increasing fees generated by 12% by bringing 2 additional outside divisions into the audit) and so on and so on. **There is no field of professional endeavor that is not quantifiable.**

And that's because, at its core, business itself is quantified. Business professionals get paid in a quantified number of dollars, by a company with quantified revenue, expenses and profitability, with a quantified number of customers, vendors, and partners who either increase or decrease their interaction with the company in the course of 12 months, at a level of satisfaction that is either higher or lower.

Every role in every field is quantifiable because every topic in every area of every aspect of business is quantifiable. And the more effectively you convey that in your resume, the more persuasively you'll demonstrate that you've earned the right to the interview.

I have never seen a resume with too many numbers. If yours is the first, tweet me @cenedella.

Dinosaurs have changed a lot since you were a kid

I'm the father to three young kids, one of the surprises of which has been how much dinosaurs have changed since I was a kid. Brontosaurus is no more, T. Rex crouches forward like a chicken instead of staggering lopsided like Godzilla, and fully half of the favorites today weren't known when I was growing up.

Yep, dinosaurs have changed a lot since I was a kid.

Which shows you that even events from 100 million years ago can change in a few decades.

Similarly, just because you graduated college a decade or more ago, doesn't mean you can't change your college experience to match your resume needs today. While you can't fake fossils, or credits, you should recast your educational history to support your professional endeavors.

• Minimized customer complaints and increased sales by xx% by restructuring...
EDUCATION
Grad School University Name   2001
Master's in Precisely Specific Degree, Houston, TX
• Winner of award, distinction or honor
• Member of club, society, or organization
Undergraduate College or University Name, Austin, TX   1999
BS/BA in Precisely Specific Degree
• Winner of award, distinction or honor
PERSONAL PATENTS AWARDS TECHNOLOGIES KEYWORDS (OPTIONAL)

Remember that your resume isn't about which 2 or 3 activities you enjoyed most at school or derived the most satisfaction from. It's about listing the 2 or 3 most important things to your future boss, and which are most likely to get you an interview.

You can make your education from the past support your pitch today:
- Highlight coursework that supports your present career. For example, if you were a finance and engineering double major, but chose to pursue one or other professionally, you'd be best advised to use the scarce real estate on your resume to highlight the relevant major rather than giving equal space to both.
- Dinosaur names have changed and so has the lingo since your college days. Update lingo and terminology to be in line with today's usage. Apatosaurus rules, brontosaurus drools.
- Rather than listing the clubs you enjoyed most, list the clubs most relevant to your current career path.

As with titles, it's mandatory that you be precise with degree names, levels, fields, and dates. If you received a B.A. in History in 1999 from Colby College, don't inflate, alter, or add to the facts. The higher you go, the more scrupulous you'll need to be about correcting errors as well. If an errant bio starts describing your B.A. in History as a B.S. in History of Science, it is up to you to proactively correct it. Because only you will bear the punishment if it's caught and corrected by someone else.

As for bullets in education, the farther out of school you are, the less contemporary professional value your degree confers, so the number of bullet points should be proportionately small. After 10 years, three bullet points to cover clubs, awards, and academics, is the most you should entertain.

Please don't use graphics on your resume

Please don't use graphics on your resume.

If you are an artist, graphic designer, visual artist or professional in the media of television, film or internet, don't.

And if you're a professional in any field that does **not** have visual communication as its work product, don't.

If you're a professional in the United States of America, Canada, or any North American country, don't include graphics or images on your resume.

For everyone else, do not use graphics on your resume. Here are the reasons why.

People's tastes differ. You may think it's attractive, your reader may not. Readers of your resume who mildly like, or even moderately approve of, your graphics choice, will not look more favorably on your ability to do their job as a result. There is nothing in their incentives, practices, or outcomes that encourages them to do so.

And the people who strongly dislike or even modestly disapprove of, your choice of graphics, are being turned away from your advertisement for a reason that has nothing to do with your experience. With so little to gain, and everything to lose, why bother adding graphics to your resume?

Of your four audiences, the computerized ATS likes graphics the least, frequently mangling them and the surrounding resume irretrievably — it's like gum on your shoe for an ATS.

None of your four audiences are grading you on the aesthetic qualities of your resume. It's simply not on the list of important factors in screening or interviewing. And none of their bosses reward them for finding people with graphical resumes.

Standard resume templates do not include graphics for a reason. If it had come to the attention of resume writers, and readers, over time that a slight dash of color or a clever use of pattern along the edges made a resume more attractive, the practice would have become widespread. But as these flourishes add little, and potentially distract substantially, from the goal of a resume, they've not been adopted.

The benefits you bring to your boss should stand out, your resume format shouldn't. Your resume is not a place to be creative. As the type of person who pays a few bucks for a resume guide, you're probably not the type that wants to use the blank resume page as a canvas for your creative endeavors. But you might be. And this is not the place.

How many SEO experts does it take to change a light bulb, lightbulb, light, bulb, lamp, lighting, switch?

On the topic of design, however, there is one item, perhaps surprising, to learn and master. Because of the way Google, or any search engine really, consumes information, certain new and odd practices have arisen in the modern era. And that means keywords.

In the usual course of creating your resume, you've already used a host of keywords and key phrases without knowing it. "Brand management", "cost containment", "integrated testing", "contract drafting" and more.

Your target audience uses keywords to find you, so you'll need to use keywords to be found. This isn't surprising. Modern search is so good because it understands the value of how humans naturally describe, or search for, things.

If I asked you to search Google for people in your field using the phrase "people who know…", what are the first thirty terms you'd type? It could be tasks, software programs, systems that you use, activities you undertake, or any nouns that are relevant to your job. Typically, you'll find that you already have fifteen to twenty of these mentioned on your resume without additional effort.

PERSONAL, PATENTS, AWARDS, TECHNOLOGIES, KEYWORDS (OPTIONAL)

Team Leadership Award 2018, Certified Manager (CM), Conflict Management Certified (CCM), 3x Employee of the Year (2018, 2016, 2014), Process Improvement Category 2015, JustFood ERP, NetSuite, Prodsmart, IQMS ERP Software, Integrify, Deskera ERP Software, Risk Mitigation, Research & Development, Profit & Loss, Lean Manufacturing, JIT, TQM, Purchasing & Supply Chain Management, Change Agent, Production Cultivation, Production Harvest, XtraCHEF, Parsley, FiiX, ProLease Maintenance, SiteDocs

Firstname I. Lastname

It's a case of "see and be seen". None of the computer software systems that parse resumes are particularly discerning with regard to placement on the page, so the distinction between a word or phrase appearing in the last bullet of your last job and it appearing in your professional summary is actually rather small, or in many cases, zero.

If you're able to work these thirty into the body of your text, in a natural way, that's terrific. But if you weren't able to, use this Personal, Patents, Awards, Technologies and Keywords section at the end of your resume to include as many as possible.

In our resume example above, we've packed in patents, names of software programs, Employee of the Year awards, and skills that are important, but not important enough to make it into the professional summary. All of these assist in getting the resume found during keyword searches.

Don't overlook the fundamentals here either. I was helping a friend who is a senior technology manager with her resume last year, and while she'd listed all the latest and greatest, cutting edge, stuff, she'd forgotten to list the basics, such as MySQL and Python. These are really the beginning stepping stones in her field, and her knowledge of the more advanced software clearly implied that she'd mastered these two technologies as well... but only to someone experienced in the field, such as a hiring manager. And by assuming it was obvious, my friend forgot that the 23-year-old screener who does the first pass through the resumes might not know these evident facts.

Your 23-year-old screener may not understand your field either. So use the Keywords section to load up on the basics. The important thing is to think through the thirty or so different ways that a future boss, or recruiter, or screener might want to find you and ensure that all of those phrases, keywords, or nouns make an appearance on your resume. It will help make sure your resume does not accidentally get overlooked.

One resume to rule them all

You've got one resume, four audiences, and one goal: to get the interview.

Inevitably, you too will be tempted, not by a golden ring, but by the desire to create multiple resumes. This tactic is not worth your time.

You've got one message -- I'm an experienced professional in my field and I'm worth an interview because the variety of achievements in my past roles match up, more or less, with a job that you are currently recruiting for. Perhaps more, perhaps less, but within the acceptable range of possibility.

To successfully tailor a resume for each type of job you're pursuing requires that you understand each set of audiences with precision, craft your resume with enough insight into what they're specifically looking for, prevent your various resume versions from falling into the wrong hands, and maintaining a public internet and social media presence precisely consistent with each resume you customize.

It's not possible. It's not practical.

You've got four audiences that your resume is addressing in the hopes of attracting that interview. Conceptually, then, your multiple resumes need to appeal not to four audiences, but to eight, twelve, or more, audiences. Let's recap who those audiences are:

The resume screener who "bars and stars"; the recruiter for whom "your reflected glow shines back on me"; the computer, "see and be seen"; and the hiring manager who asks "is the sum total person likely to be able to make me look good next year."

First, the 23-year-old screener who "bars and stars." She's simply trying to understand if you make the cut. The level of nuance that it takes for her to understand the difference between the sub-fields or sub-categories in your field is beyond the scope of her duties, role, and capabilities. If you pass the **bar**, you get the **star**. Multiple resumes don't provide an advantage with the screener.

Next, the recruiter. For the recruiter, he's looking to craft a story about you. If the job is for one specialty in your field, and you're currently employed in the other, he'll make that connection for the hiring manager. With their tendency towards over-inclusion, diverse experience is a good thing, not a drawback. Multiple resumes don't help with this audience either.

And for the hiring manager, who understands the full nuance involved, it's a 50-50 chance that they're looking for someone with broader, rather than more narrow, experience. So your multiple resume strategy doesn't appreciably alter your odds here.

For the ATS's, it's "see and be seen." If the words are on the resume, it doesn't quite matter as strongly as the particular arrangement. The ATS is simply going to chop up your resume into the component keywords and phrases and store those in a database somewhere. Then, whenever someone searches for those keywords, they'll return your resume. When it comes to the computerized software systems, having multiple resumes doesn't particularly matter.

As your goal with the resume is to land the interview, crafting multiple resumes provides relatively little upside potential, and the strategy comes with too many risks in management, writing and time management.

In fact, the only audience that likes multiple resumes is you. Like an actor trying out for a part, you're trying on different costumes, different roles, different makeup, to see if you like how you look.

My experience over the last two decades suggests:
- Your four audiences are not paying enough attention to make the differences meaningful. As our own research has shown, small changes in word emphasis are lost on the typical resume reviewer. They spend 7 seconds doing a first review of your resume. Get the big picture right, and good things follow. If you waste time wordsmithing, you'll frustrate yourself.
- It's very difficult for you to appreciate the subtle differences between what different sets of audiences want, specifically.

And trying to create a resume without knowing the specifics of what the audience thinks is like trying to do golf club selection without seeing where on the course your ball lies.
- You don't have the time to become a great resume writer. Perhaps a great writer could communicate these subtle nuances, if she had enough experience with the audience, the material, and the intended effect. You don't want to invest the time to become a great resume writer, you want your next job. Focus your efforts on where you can make the most impact.
- You're too close to yourself, and too far from understanding the market for professionals like you, to craft the right message. Your target audience has reviewed dozens of resumes for this very position. As a result, your audience has a much more nuanced and subtle feel for what the market looks like and which experiences and backgrounds are big advantages. It's simply unlikely that even a great writer will guess correctly what each particular reviewer wants to see most. You are far better off getting a single resume "mostly right" and investing the rest of your job-search time elsewhere.
- Opportunities for routine errors multiply as you manage multiple documents. You're going through enough without juggling different resume files.
- And finally, it is difficult to keep multiple resumes consistent with your online presence. The public web is not segmentable -- your public search and social media profiles are available to one and all. As your social media presence looks the same to each of your audiences, regardless of which resume you've provided them, you've taken on the

additional difficult task of keeping each resume version consistent with your public persona. If the two look dissimilar, or, even worse, conflict in small or important ways, you set yourself apart as an unserious, or potentially, untruthful, candidate. Nothing will get you unhired faster than untruths.

Among the various resume-related activities in which you could invest your time, creating multiple resumes is your lowest ROI.

Don't customize your resume for each job or company, customize your pitch and your interview using the same resume document. Professionals should not try to craft different resumes for each company, rather, they should craft different stories for each company, based on the same resume document.

One presence, one theme, one summary, one coherent career goal...

One resume to rule them all.

Putting your resume to work

Well, we've come to the end of our time together here in *Ladders 2019 Resume Guide.*

I hope you've found it helpful.

I also hope you've seen that writing resumes is not mysterious, but rather can be educational and even entertaining. Developing a deeper understanding of ourselves and the market for our work can only make us more capable as professionals. A resume is a document that is intended to make your life easier at the same time that it clarifies to future bosses how you're best able to succeed.

If you're like most American professionals that I've come across as Founder of Ladders, you want to do work similar to your current work but at a new place and a new level. To do so, you need to explain to strangers, with confidence, how you will be able to contribute to the new team. You need a professional advertisement.

We started from the outside in, exploring the "how come" of resumes. We redefined the resume in a way that makes it both more powerful, as well as easier to understand as a business document: "Your resume is a professional advertisement, targeted toward your future boss, with the goal of landing an interview for a job that you can succeed in."

I mentioned that you can find additional information on the homepage for this book:
https://www.theladders.com/career-advice/resume-guide

And that we've uploaded 73 separate resume templates for you to use in your own resume writing, on Ladders' website here:
https://www.theladders.com/resume-examples

I hope you'll find both resources useful.

We discussed how the top third of your resume is sacred space. In the past you've tried to convey all sorts of messages with that part of your resume. You've wanted to convey something important about your character **and** your abilities **and** your many, many different skills **and** your flexibility **and** your background **and** your educational attainments **and** your recognition in the community **and** too many things!

FIRSTNAME I. LASTNAME

firstname.lastname.2019@gmail.com
Address - City - State - Zip Code
(212) 555-1212

GENERAL & OPERATIONS MANAGER

COO • VP, Ops & Admin • Country Manager • Senior Operations Director
Business Development • Revenue Generation • Strategic Planning • Relationship Management
Led Business Growth • Increased Productivity • Reduced Costs • Effective Recruiter
Team Leadership Award 2018 • 3x Executive of the Year • Promoted Early • Public Speaker

WORK EXPERIENCE

Current Company Name, Inc., New York, NY   **April 2015 - present**
Chief Operating Officer
Leading Contract Manufacturer in Service Industry
- Increased productivity by xx% after taking over supply...
- Delivered 3 new distribution centres on budget...
- Improved results for delivery success goals by xx%...
- Optimized sourcing strategies resulting in 8 new manufacturing...
- Produced savings of $xx million across operations, maintenance...
- Reduced defects by over xx% by implementing large-scale...
- Generated a xx% on-time performance increase by streamlining...
- Exceeded market share goal by x points through reduction of...

Prior Company, Inc., Lake Forest, IL   **Jan 2011 - April 2015**
General & Operations Manager
$14 Billion Global Manufacturer and Distributor
- Maximized profitability, generating over $xx million annually by implementing...
- Accelerated delivery of new technologies to reduce headcount by 16%, adding...
- Achieved xx days reduction in closing cycle time by overseeing analysis of...
- Sold 3 data centers, generating $xx million in cost reductions...
- Decreased technical and operational costs by xx% by creating strategies...
- Orchestrated xx% revenue growth by developing and executing...
- Streamlined logistics resulting in $xx million in annual cost savings...
- Grew net income by more than xxx% by overseeing...

You've learned instead that the professional summary at the top of your resume is your billboard. It's where you assert who you will be, and what you bring to your future employer.

125

You'll show your four audiences, using your professional summary, who you are, what job you want, and why you're qualified for it.

Your bullet points support the argument you're making in the professional summary. Viewing each bullet point as a pillar in your case, you'll quantify your ability to generate success for your future boss. The easiest way to do that is to share numerical data that demonstrates how you've contributed in the past and can, therefore, contribute in the future. Every bullet point is an investment. Use them to powerfully drive your points home.

We reviewed in detail the four audiences for your resume, how they're similar and how they're different. You've learned the importance of being straightforward to get past the junior screener; to provide the keywords and key accomplishments that entice a recruiter; to detail your background with success verbs and a number to impress the future boss; and to keep it simple so that the computer systems don't bite you.

I hope that understanding how a resume is put together will help you better understand how your career is put together. When you can see your own professional track record and possibilities in the same way that recruiters, hiring managers, and your future bosses see them, you'll be more effective at pushing your career in the direction you want. Knowledge of the path and obstacles in front of you will only improve your ability to take advantage of them.

Middle Company, Inc., City of Industry, CA   2004 - 2011
Promoted early from Product Manager
General & Operations Manager   **May 2007 - Jan 2011**
- Added 310 basis points to customer satisfaction scores by...
- Gained xx% efficiency improvement by implementing...
- Contributed to a budgetary saving of $xxM through the acquisition...
- Expanded role to supervision of 5 critical distribution locations...

Product Manager   **Sep 2004 - May 2007**
Operational Product Management
- Awarded patent for osmosis system that reduced costs by 67% in core manufacturing...
- Eliminated 12% of components through product redesign while maintaining quality...
- Introduced a pricing strategy that saw a xx% rise in increased...

First Company, Inc., San Antonio, TX   **July 2001 - Sep 2004**
Product Manager
Strategic Product Management at Global Industrial Manufacturer
- Saved 23% on operating costs by implementing ordering...
- Minimized customer complaints and increased sales by xx% by restructuring...

EDUCATION
Grad School University Name   2001
Master's in Precisely Specific Degree, Houston, TX
- Winner of award, distinction or honor
- Member of club, society, or organization

Undergraduate College or University Name, Austin, TX   1999
BS/BA in Precisely Specific Degree
- Winner of award, distinction or honor

PERSONAL, PATENTS, AWARDS, TECHNOLOGIES, KEYWORDS (OPTIONAL)

Team Leadership Award 2018, Certified Manager (CM), Conflict Management Certified (CCM), 3x Employee of the Year (2018, 2016, 2014), Process Improvement Category 2015, JustFood ERP, NetSuite, Prodsmart, IQMS ERP Software, Integrify, Deskera ERP Software, Risk Mitigation, Research & Development, Profit & Loss, Lean Manufacturing, JIT, TQM, Purchasing & Supply Chain Management, Change Agent, Production Cultivation, Production Harvest, XtraCHEF, Parsley, FiiX, ProLease Maintenance, SiteDocs

Firstname I. Lastname

A resume is a professional advertisement and should be used to advertise. That means it's time to get it out there and put your resume into the hands of your intended audience. We cover strategies to do just that in *Ladders 2019 Job Search Guide* and *Ladders 2019 Networking Guide*.

We've spent a couple hours together and I hope you feel much more empowered with regard to your resume, now and in the future. Overall, the resume writing guide in the prior pages is remarkably simple because the job search process, despite all the anxiety and confusion, is remarkably simple.

When you share your goals and desired job titles, along with the specific data and numbers that indicate you can succeed in the role, you make it easy for screeners, recruiters, and hiring managers to invite you to join them for your next great role in life.

I wish you the best of luck with your resume writing and your resume sharing and all your future successes.

I'm rooting for you!

More best practices & advice online

For more free information, templates, and tools to help with your resume, visit:

www.theladders.com/career-advice/resume-guide
www.theladders.com/free-resume-templates
www.theladders.com/resume-examples

Find us on Facebook:

www.facebook.com/LaddersHQ/

About the Author

Marc Cenedella is Founder and CEO of Ladders, Inc., the $100K+ careers site. *Marc's Monday Newsletter*, reaching 10 million readers weekly, is America's largest career advice newsletter.

A nationally renowned thought leader on job search, career management and recruiting, Marc is frequently sought out by national media organizations for his expert commentary on employment and entrepreneurialism. He has been profiled in The New York Times, Wall Street Journal, Fortune, Wired, and Businessweek, appeared on CNN, Fox News, MSNBC, CNBC, and Bloomberg.

Made in the USA
Middletown, DE
29 April 2019